Zoë has been my close and trusted friend for twenty-two years. Throughout that time she has always been a dedicated campaigner and pioneer. She has tirelessly walked with me through my own baby loss, from beginning to end, offering not only support in a professional capacity but also an unparalleled understanding, having gone through the journey herself. Nothing is ever too much for her. As a highly respected leader Zoë has become a trailblazer in changing the culture and care surrounding baby loss and grief, not only within the UK but globally. This has led her to be a voice to the media and government (which even gave her the privilege of holding a private reception at 10 Downing Street), and receiving national honours at the House of Lords. I was proud to attend and see first-hand the impact of this event.

This book cements her standing as a beacon of hope around the world, and for anyone who has suffered baby loss, it will make the world of difference. Don't just buy one, buy ten, and give them to people you know; I know I will be!

Beth Redman, Wife, Mother, Singer, Author, Speaker and Campaigner for Change

For those who have been through the tragic loss of a child, this book provides step-by-step help and advice to work through and process grief and trauma. Knowing Zoë personally, I can honestly say that there is no one better placed to walk you through the grieving process.

Jo Hemmings, Behavioural Psychologist & Media Personality

Baby loss tragically affects hundreds of thousands of people each year in the UK, causing trauma, pain, grief, feelings of isolation and much more. As a Director and leader within the midwifery profession, I have seen first-hand how this affects people's lives, and how the right advice and support are invaluable in helping a person come to terms with their loss. Zoë bravely shares her personal story of heartbreak and loss, and then compassionately gives that daily support people so often need. It takes people by the hand, acknowledges their pain and their unique circumstances, and gives wisdom in how to get through each day, a day at a time. I cannot recommend this book enough; it will be a source of strength to many women, their partners and families.

Dr Jacque Gerrard MSc, RGN, RM,
Director Royal College of Midwives England

The tragedy and trauma of losing a baby changes us forever. Zoë has used her personal experience of five losses to deliver a book that demonstrates a deep understanding and compassion to all who are grieving. I am pleased to call Zoë a friend, and wholeheartedly recommend this book to anyone who wants to find support and hope.

Kym Marsh, Actor and Singer/Songwriter

Zoë is an inspirational lady, who talks with truth, honesty and compassion on an issue that affects us all. We are all part of communities, friendship groups, families who have been through or are going through miscarriage and infant loss, and this amazing book is such a beautiful way of reaching, teaching and helping us. Please read this book daily and know you are not on your own in your thoughts, fears and grief.

Anna Smith, Author and Speaker

SAYING GOODBYE

ZOË CLARK-COATES

A personal story of baby loss and 90 days
of support to walk you through grief

Marino Branch
Brainse Marino
Tel: 8336297

David C Cook
transforming lives together

SAYING GOODBYE Published by David C Cook, 4050 Lee Vance Drive
Colorado Springs, CO 80918, U.S.A.

Integrity Music Ltd., a division of David C Cook, Eastbourne, East Sussex
BN23 6NT, United Kingdom

ISBN 978-1-4347-1226-4

The Cook Team: Ian Matthews, Jennie Pollock, Jo Stockdale

Cover Design: Mark Prentice, beatroot.media

Cover image: Adobe stock

Typesetting by Zaccmedia

Printed in the United Kingdom

First Edition 2017
0 1 2 3 4 5 6 7 8 9 10

Contents

Foreword

O ver 250,000 babies are going to die in the UK this year and thirty-eight million globally. I was horrified when I heard that. All that pain. 'Someone's got to do something!' I thought, mouth full of biscuit, 'Petition someone! The government or someone! The UN? The World Health Organization? Can these numbers be reduced? Are those mothers getting any care or support?'

Zoë Clark-Coates knows only too well the pain of baby loss, having gone through this tragedy five times, but rather than just becoming a statistic and sitting back in a mush of self-pity and eating her own weight in biscuits as I did after baby loss, she has become a vocal campaigner for change. As the founder and CEO of The Mariposa Trust (also known as 'Saying Goodbye', the name of its principal division), which in just four years has become a leading international support charity, she has been instrumental in elevating the issue of baby loss onto a national platform, and revolutionising baby loss support. As a trained counsellor, writer, broadcaster and business and charity CEO, she leads a team of over 240 people who provide support that reaches over fifty thousand people each week globally.

She has two young girls, the first born after three losses, and the second born after a further two losses, so she's really ridden that childbearing rollercoaster and knows the jubilation, but also the loss, fear and grief that too often come along too. Her personal experience makes her the most empathetic of companions as she understands the effect baby loss can have on people mentally, emotionally and physically. I cannot recommend this book highly enough.

In this book, Zoë has opened up about her story of pain, loss and hope, and provides a ninety-day plan, including words of support, and practical advice to help you through the months following a bereavement. Each day has words of encouragement, hope, peace and comfort as well as hands-on tips for getting through the darkest of days, and finding hope.

I believe that this book is a must-have for anyone who suffers baby loss, for anyone who has been through baby loss in the past, or for those wishing to gain a greater insight into the trauma of loss. You'll find here some of the powerful truths that you or those you love need to hear, and help to dispel the untruths surrounding baby loss, which often cloud this taboo subject. For many people, this will not just be a gift, this will be a lifeline.

Sally Phillips.
May 2017

Introduction

F irst and foremost, this book is for those who have lost a baby. It is for those who want to feel understood, and for those who are looking for their feelings to be validated. Sadly, we live in a time where we are encouraged to put all our feelings in a box and then only to open this box at set times, but life just isn't like that.

Life can be hard. It can be wonderful. And it can be traumatising. I hope this book encourages you to be real about your story, and gives you time and space to reflect and heal.

This book is also for family members, friends and health professionals who want to gain a true insight into losing a baby. If you have not experienced it first-hand, you will not be able to relate to all you read here, but it should allow you to glimpse this painful world, and to be compassionate to those who have had to live in it.

Chapter 1 Zoë's Story

Where do I even start when writing a story like this? This question has been a constant niggle for the past few weeks. In theory, it should be simple to write down my experiences, but in practice, it is hard. I am afraid I cannot write eloquently. I am nervous of digging back into past traumas, even though I know I have processed and dealt with them all. I am also scared of being utterly vulnerable, of laying it all out in one book. For a private person that is a big ask, and I am extremely private. But I know that if this book helps just one person, it will be worth it. So here goes.

Let's start at the very beginning (yes, I know that sounds like *The Sound of Music* … sorry about that, there are far fewer hills and dance sequences in the pages that follow).

Andy and I were thirty-two when we decided we would like to have children. We had always planned to have children, but it was never something that consumed us. We felt complete as a couple.

I don't remember what flicked that switch, when we went from being okay with the idea of having children 'one day', to passionately wanting them immediately, but there was a change, and it happened in us both simultaneously. One thing that had definitely delayed the decision was that one of my closest friends had lost multiple children through miscarriage and stillbirth. This had left a scar on me. I didn't feel I could handle that type of loss or depth of grief. But once we made the decision to try for a baby the fear left me. My sister had never lost a child, so why would I, when we were from the same family?

Within months I realised I was pregnant. I was so excited, and even though I was nervous of the changes ahead, I was overjoyed.

And then the bleeding started. I knew I was losing the baby. I believed early miscarriage would be just like a normal period, maybe a bit heavier, but it wasn't. It was agony. For six days, I was in horrendous pain and the blood loss was huge. Emotionally, I could not handle it. I found it hard to say 'I am miscarrying', so I dealt with the physical symptoms and shoved all other emotions into a box.

We told no one about our baby. We hardly discussed anything even between ourselves. I preferred to stay in a state of denial: it felt much easier than having to face the pain.

We named this baby Cobi.

The months that followed went slow. The irony was not lost on me that you spend your adult life not wanting to get pregnant and trying to avoid it, and as soon as you want a child you realise how hard it is to actually conceive. You constantly hear about this teenager and that lady over the road who has found themselves pregnant, and it being the worst thing in the world for them, and you think 'What? How is it possible that so many can create a child they don't even want, and yet here we are desperately trying, and it's not happening?'

I felt lied to by every biology teacher I have ever had, every film I had seen where two people decide to have a child and it happens on the first night they try. Making a baby is not like that. It is like the most complex science experiment ever … plus a gazillion other things needing to be in place at that exact moment. One massive star to be hovering in the east, the moon being a perfect crescent, and the sun radiating at 91 degrees, and just to be on the safe side drink the fresh milk from a goat born in the west… Well, maybe that's an exaggeration, but that's what it feels like. Many things have to happen for that egg to be fertilised, and many more for that egg to then implant and start growing. Studying the complexity of creating a child amazes me. It truly is a miracle when a baby is conceived.

But then …

It happened …

I weed on that ever-knowing stick, and two lines appeared.

(Can I just add here that it seems somewhat too personal to say I weed on a stick? Does urinated sound better? No, I simply can't have the word urinated in my book—we need to stick with wee—but we all wee, right? Maybe not on sticks, but it is a normal human function!)

I was pregnant.

This time it felt different. I was scared of losing this baby, but I also felt it was protected. The early weeks are so challenging in pregnancy as there is nothing you can do to make sure things are fine. Scans can help a little, but until your baby has a heartbeat, no one can reassure you that all is well, so you are left feeling helpless. All you can do is take your pregnancy vitamins and eat well. I did both, and started searching for a doctor.

Both excited and nervous, we went to meet the obstetrician I had found. He was lovely and we felt we would be in safe hands.

He asked me if I would like a scan whilst I was there and we leapt at the chance to see our baby. This was to be my first ever scan so I was not too sure of what to expect but the sonographer (a lovely Australian) swiftly applied the gel to my stomach and the scan commenced. She asked if we were sure our dates were correct, which made my stomach flip, but we said yes, and she agreed with us.

She said she could see I had previously had a bleed, which had been retained in the womb. If I started to bleed following the scan, I shouldn't worry as it would just be this blood being evacuated. She asked us if we would like to hear the baby's heartbeat. The sound filled the room. We both shed a tear or two. It was such a beautiful moment seeing our child on that screen and hearing their heart pounding away.

A few hours later, at home, I went to the loo and noticed some spotting. I wanted to vomit from fear but Andy calmed me down, reminding we had been warned this could happen and that I should not worry if it did. The bleeding was just random spotting and, after a few days, it stopped.

As Christmas was approaching, we decided not to tell anyone we were pregnant and started to plan a big surprise for the whole family. No one would ever guess we would keep something like this from them. They had all stopped asking us if we would have children, once we had been married for over ten years, so we knew this would be completely unexpected.

We planned a treasure hunt on Christmas Eve for all the family. Each would be given separate clues, and would end up in a different place where they would discover one of the many positive pregnancy test sticks I had. (When you're struggling to conceive, it can be hard to believe the evidence of just one test. I had at least five positives.) We were both so excited and wondered how everyone would react.

I then caught the dreaded flu. I started with a fever and sore throat and before long was bed-ridden. I hardly moved for five days and decided my first outing would just be a quick visit to the shop.

I am known for having a bladder made of steel and can go for over ten hours without needing to use the loo, but within days of discovering I was pregnant, I was spending a lot of time popping to the loo. It was no surprise then that mid-shop I had to find a staff member and beg them to let me use their facilities. There I discovered I was bleeding.

I wanted to pass out. Sweat was pouring off me, and I felt so nauseous I could hardly move. Andy and I walked out of the shop and climbed into the car.

We called the hospital who told us we should find a more local clinic to scan me, as travelling is not advised when bleeding in pregnancy. Andy started phoning private clinics, as we knew the NHS would not be able to offer me an instant scan.

After a handful of phone calls, Andy found a small clinic whose obstetrician would happily see me if we could get there within the hour.

On arrival, we were greeted by a friendly woman, and given many forms to fill in. As we sat and waited, all we could think was, 'Is our baby okay?'

My name was called and we were led into a large office. Gel was applied to my tummy, the screen was switched on and the monitor turned towards us. Instantly we could see our baby was fine. The heartbeat was strong and our little treasure was waving away.

I sobbed with relief. The doctor said he could not see why I was bleeding, but that it was more common to bleed in pregnancy than not to, which did reassure us somewhat.

As a precaution, I chose to rest until the bleeding stopped, only getting up to help at a Christmas event we had planned with the neighbours on the Saturday night.

So around 5pm, I got out of bed. As I moved, I felt the bleeding increase. I started to weep uncontrollably. I screamed to God and begged Him to save my child. I felt truly terrified and out of control. I knew in my heart my baby had just died. How? Mother's instinct? God telling me? I do not know, but I knew her heart had just stopped. I wailed, I begged and I implored God to start her heart and save her.

Neither Andy nor I knew what to do next. Our event was waiting to start, we could see around thirty people lingering at the rear of our house, and many more would soon be there. Andy told some friends of ours, Nick and Georgina, what was happening and asked them to take the reins. They were marvellous, agreed to take over and shared with Andy how they had gone through a similar experience when pregnant with their second son. They also offered to talk with me. They advised us to go to A&E and to phone ahead to warn them we were coming.

I anticipated a chaotic A&E as it was a Saturday night, but all was calm, too early in the evening for all the drink-fuelled accidents. I told the receptionist why we were there—I don't know why I expected empathy but I did. I was petrified, and I wanted them to appreciate that. I wanted them to see a mum to be, desperately trying to save her child. But I was just told to take a seat and wait to be called.

Eventually my name was called and I was led to a cubicle. The young nurse assigned to look after me seemed nice but confused as to what to do next. Once she had taken a urine sample to test, she announced, 'Great. You're still pregnant!'

Silence descended. She then asked, 'Can I ask why you are so upset? Is it because this is an IVF baby, so you have paid a lot for it?'

I couldn't speak, and felt utterly ridiculous. Clearly I was crying more than she thought I should, for a baby that had no value because we had not paid for her.

Eventually I managed to say, 'No, this baby was conceived naturally!'

'Oh, okay,' she said.

She said no scans would be available until the following Friday so all I could do was go home and wait, rest and presume all was fine.

We headed home.

Our world was very different now. I had a spark of hope that maybe this bleed was insignificant but the overriding feeling was that my baby had died. I woke on the Sunday morning feeling tired and petrified. My night had been filled with nightmares, replays of the day before.

We wanted to get a scan at another clinic as there was no way I was waiting until the Friday for answers, but they were all closed on Sundays. We left countless messages on voicemails asking for a call back as soon as they opened. The day dragged as I flitted between hope and hopelessness.

One minute I felt our baby was fine and it was just fear convincing me she had died. The next, I was overwhelmed with terror. We felt utterly helpless.

On Monday morning, a local clinic offered a scan if we could get there within the next couple of hours. I knew I could not carry on any longer without telling my parents and my sister. Our big surprise seemed unlikely now, and I needed the support only a mum and a sister can give.

I called my parents, one of the hardest calls I have ever made. It was beyond awful to say I was pregnant, but that I thought the baby had died.

I sobbed. My parents sobbed. They said they would come. Then I called Hayley, my sister. We wept, and she tried to reassure me. Then we left for the clinic, and drove in silence, as tears rolled down my face. The clinic was warm and welcoming, and a midwife performed the scan. She seemed quiet, but kind.

To our surprise the images were played onto a massive TV screen. There our baby was, in all her beauty. But she was so still. The midwife activated the sound on the scanner to listen to her heart. You could hear a pin drop in the silence.

'Why can't I hear her heart beating?'

The midwife looked at me and said, 'Zoë, I am so sorry. Your baby has died.'

If I thought I was free-falling before, now I felt I had been pushed off the side of the earth.

Chapter 2

How could this have happened?

The midwife left the room. Andy and I cried and clung to each other. Minutes later, the midwife re-entered the room, followed by a tall man with a powerful presence. He was one of the two obstetricians who owned the clinic. He then said words which we would quickly become accustomed to: 'I am so sorry your baby has died.'

He had seen the scan in his office, so he already knew what the midwife had told us was accurate.

We were shown to a room where we could sit quietly. We cried, and I was shaking uncontrollably.

'What do we do now?' we both asked.

Time stood still. Seconds felt endless.

Eventually I said we needed to call my parents and let them know. I shakily dialled their number, and as soon as they answered, I said, 'Our baby's died, she doesn't have a heartbeat.'

Mum wept down the phone with me. We then called Hayley and told her the same news.

I begged the clinic to rescan and they kindly agreed. This scan showed the same, but it helped me to see it was not just a terrible mistake.

The midwife said we could wait for nature to take its course or we could have a medical intervention. She advised us to have another scan in two to three days to see how things were, and to confirm that she had died.

'Have you ever done a scan days later and the baby has suddenly been okay?'

She said she had read of a case once but never seen it personally. That little bit of information gave me a strand of hope to hold onto.

As I hate being treated in hospitals, we decided the best course of action would be to have a natural delivery at home. At least we could go home and be together as a family. It felt like the best decision.

We walked out into a very different world.

We were definitely in shock, but not enough to be numb. The pain was raw, sharp and agonising. It hurt to breathe, to speak, even just to be. The thought of walking into our home was almost impossible, so we went to our neighbours' house and told them what had happened. They offered us comfort and much needed support.

As the time approached for my parents to arrive, we went home. We waited for my mum and dad, hoping they could make everything okay. Isn't it funny how even at the ages we were, we believed my mum and dad could magically make it all fine?

I will never forget the looks on their faces when they walked into our sitting room. Mum was pale and crying. Dad crumpled as he looked at me and I saw him openly sob for maybe the third time in my life. This was one of the worst moments. It wasn't just that we were in agony; my whole family was heartbroken. We told them the complete story.

I did not know what to do with myself and would often just pace the room or sit on a chair, looking out at all the neighbours' Christmas lights twinkling in the darkness, saying to my mum that none of it made sense. How could we be living this nightmare?

At such times, words seem futile, so you just sit in silence listening to the sounds of life: a freezer buzzing in the background, or traffic outside.

The next day my parents suggested visiting my grandparents. They were desperate to see us after hearing the news, and mum thought a trip out the house might be helpful.

I could hardly utter a word. That slight numbing feeling had completely worn off, and my grief was at its rawest.

To break the silence in the car Andy turned the radio on. Minutes from my grandparents' house a song came on, *The First Time Ever I Saw Your Face* by Leona Lewis—the song we had planned to have playing when I gave birth.

In that exact moment the pain I experienced was so terrible, there are no words to describe it. I screamed a silent scream, one only a parent who has lost a child can make.

We pulled onto my grandparents' drive, and my parents went into the house. Andy helped me out of the car, and I fell into his arms, screaming. Only when I stopped violently shaking and crying did we walk into the house.

My grandparents both told us how sorry they were.

I simply nodded. I then sat in silence.

A few hours later we drove home.

The following day was the day of the scan.

The whole of the previous evening I had been praying over my baby bump, begging God to make her heart start beating again. I believe in miracles, so however mad this may sound to someone who does not believe in God, I truly believed it was possible to be rescanned, and to be told a mistake had been made and she was now fine. I could almost imagine myself standing up at an event sharing this amazing story of how God had saved my child. Therefore, whilst I was dreading this scan, I also believed I could walk out smiling.

This time the other resident obstetrician was doing my scan.

There she was in all her beauty on the screen but no heartbeat could be found. Our precious baby, whom we had named Darcy, was gone.

Chris, the doctor, was amazing. I could not have asked for more compassion. He held my hand and shared his own story of loss. I knew he got it and that made the world of difference.

We left the clinic grief-stricken.

At home, time crawled by.

I continued suffering with all the same pregnancy symptoms, which was really distressing. When your pregnancy is going well, all those symptoms—sickness, heartburn, aching hips, headaches—are all acceptable. They are reminders that you are pregnant, and you tell yourself it's worth it. However, once your baby has died, all of those symptoms stab your heart, reminding you of what you have lost.

However, one evening something special happened. A truly precious friendship was deepened when our friend and neighbour, Julie, came. She told me how she too had lost a child and we wept together. In that moment, she turned from a friend into a family member.

Days passed. Minutes felt like hours, hours felt like days and days felt like months.

I cried so much I often ran out of tears and would sit frozen, waiting for my tear ducts to refill and then it would start again, another endless cycle of weeping and screaming, then sitting empty and desolate.

Almost a week later, labour began. It started with mild period pain, and then it escalated. Andy sat with me as I rocked on the floor, trying to arch my back so the pain would go.

I had been waiting for this moment to arrive for the past week, but I didn't want it. I didn't want my daughter to leave my body, to be gone forever. But nothing can stop labour, and gradually the pain increased.

We became acutely aware that no one had actually told us what to expect. How much blood loss was too much? How much pain was normal?

To not know the answers whilst going through one of the worst experiences of our lives added to the trauma. We felt like the blind leading the blind.

It took twenty-four hours for our daughter to be born. The moment I delivered her, I felt empty, as if I had just lost a vital part of my body. There was no relief at all. The physical pain quickly settled but an emotional pain that was far, far worse replaced it.

The next day I sat in shock, shaking and weeping. If I managed to eat and drink anything, I felt I had accomplished enough.

A day or two later I had a scan which confirmed the only thing that remained within my womb was blood clots. So it was now officially over. I was no longer pregnant. Life could carry on as normal. The emotional pain continued and my heart remained shattered. I did not even know how to start putting my heart and my world back together.

As Christmas was now upon us, we decided to travel back with my parents to their house. It took them a while to convince us as over the previous weeks my house had become a haven, where I felt safer. But the decision turned out to be a good one.

My family surrounded us and we were allowed to be real and honest. We did not have to pretend that everything was fine. This was a massive relief. It was okay that I wept into my Christmas dinner. It was fine that I did not want to open any Christmas presents. They just let us be.

Once back home, I watched loads of programmes telling people's personal stories. I read articles of hope and bravery. Any story which showed someone had experienced heartbreak but found an inner strength to continue was a gift to me. I absorbed it all, and observed how they made their lives better. I could feel I was getting stronger.

As the weeks passed by, life did continue. We went back to work and openly told people what we had been through. I felt no shame in telling our friends, and even strangers, what we had just experienced. We were always met with compassion, and friends would sit and weep with us as we shared painful details of losing Darcy.

I will never forget meeting with Jayne, a business colleague, who over the years had become a cherished friend. We met for coffee in Selfridges in the Bullring. I told her our story and tears streamed down my face. As I looked up, Jayne was also crying. We sat weeping together, not even caring about the odd looks we were getting from passers-by. I still wonder if she knows what a gift that was to me.

The blackest, darkest part of grief was slowly lifting. I could see a light at the end of the tunnel. I learnt first-hand that all the things I had learnt when I trained as a counsellor were in fact true. Talking does help. Allowing yourself to embrace the pain you are feeling means you process things far faster. Believing and accepting there is no right or wrong way to grieve, as people are unique in their approach and feelings, gives a person a freedom to walk their own path.

I also learnt that so many common analogies of grief are also true.

Grief is like the ocean. Pain does come in waves. Sometimes those waves are huge and hit you from nowhere, knocking you off your feet. At other times, the waves are small and you can almost step over them.

But my heart was definitely healing. I could see I did have the potential to be happy again. I could imagine having more children, a huge step forward, as initially that did not seem a possibility.

Then the time came. We felt ready to try for another child. Hope was reignited. Whilst we were so scared of losing another child, we also wanted to continue with our journey with the hope that one day in the near future we would bring our child home from the hospital.

Chapter 3

So our quest for a child continued.

Were we scared? Yes. But we were more scared of never having a child to raise than we were of losing again. I had presumed loss would diminish this yearning for a child, but it did the exact opposite. It reinforced how much we wanted to be parents.

The physical effects of pregnancy slowly vanished, and I felt my body was back to normal. Emotionally I felt stable. I still had days when I was hit by a huge wave of grief, but generally, I had accepted what had happened. Allowing myself to cry whenever I felt the need really aided my heart beginning to heal.

I was now fully back to work and that helped. Whilst I was off work it reinforced the feelings of time standing still. By rejoining life and keeping busy, time passed much faster.

Anyone who goes through significant loss will also be aware of a wall that grief builds almost instantly between you and the world. It is as if you are removed from society. For some this wall is made of bricks, and they cannot even see the outside world any more, for others it is glass. My wall was always glass. I could still watch what others were doing, but I was separate from them. On one side of the wall time moved at a normal pace, and on my side things moved slowly. I constantly questioned how life for everyone else could just carry on as if nothing had happened, when on my side of the wall, a bomb had been detonated and my world lay in tatters.

By returning to work, I was able to walk around this glass wall and enter normal life again, but I constantly returned to the other side.

Then one day I woke up and the wall had gone. It was no longer me and them, I was part of life fully again. Yes, I was different, but to me that was a good thing. I did not want to be the same. To be the same 'me' would mean the children I had lost had not changed me. And they had—they had made me a mother.

Months went by. Then I got that longed for positive pregnancy test. I did not actually believe it, so did about six more. I still did not believe it.

I asked to speak privately with the pharmacist at our local chemist. We went into the discreet room at the back of the dispensing counter and I pulled out all my pregnancy test sticks, all showing varying shades of two pink lines. I said, 'Am I pregnant?' He said, 'Yes,' and burst out laughing.

When something you want so badly finally happens, it is almost impossible to accept. But there it was in black and white, or maybe more accurately in pink and white. I had to accept I was pregnant!

We were delighted.

From all I had read, and the medics I had spoken to, I was reassured that I had as much chance as the next person of having a normal, healthy pregnancy. So Andy and I made the decision to stay positive and hold onto that thread of hope with two hands.

Then I started to bleed. What was initially written off as a small pregnancy bleed quickly proved to be another miscarriage.

I went utterly numb.

The thought of telling our family and friends that we were walking this same path yet again was too much, so we decided not to. We knew no one could bring us comfort. No words could remove the pain, we had heard them all so recently, and nothing more could be said to bring us relief. All we wanted to hear was that we would definitely end up with a baby to raise, never encounter loss again, and the broken feeling would disappear. But no one could say these things.

We named the baby we lost Bailey. The weeks crawled by and the glass wall was back in place.

Up until now, I have not mentioned another member of our family—our dog Jacob, known as Jake. He was full of mischief, ruling our house, and our lives were run around his existence. He had suffered a stroke a few years prior to us starting to try for children and had pancreatitis, so we could not leave him with anyone other than my parents. We had had to carry on caring for him, all through the losses, and he filled the house with energy.

And then he had another stroke. We nursed him back to health, only to have him collapse again. The vet gave us no choice: Jake had to be put to sleep.

Minutes later, he died in our arms.

We stood in that veterinary surgery as broken people, tears streaming down our faces.

The vet kept saying, 'I am so sorry.' He knew that we had just gone through losing the babies, and did not know what to say to us.

We drove to my grandparents' house, told them what had happened, and went home.

We opened the door and were greeted with his lead, bed, toys and a very empty house. Having slept for a few hours, we knew we had to get away. We were constantly listening out for his footsteps. So we simply drove north. We hardly spoke, but sobbed and sobbed— for Cobi, for Darcy, for Bailey, our three babies, and now for Jake.

We got to the top of Scotland and knew we would have to go back. The vet would be calling to ask us to collect Jake's ashes, so we turned the car around and cried all the way home.

I was totally and utterly broken. I struggled to drink; I found it nearly impossible to eat. Life was consumed with grief.

Each night I asked God to take me to be with Him in heaven. The only way I could sleep was in the hope that I might not have to wake up again.

Each day when I woke up it took a few seconds for me to remember what we were now facing, and then it would hit me. It was like being newly bereaved each day.

Days passed and I realised I was going to have to do something to stop this cycle. There were so many things I could not change, I decided to focus on the things I could. I wanted to make our home bearable again, and the silence was reinforcing the pain of losing Jake. It also meant we had no reason to leave it—so we had to get another dog. We started visiting dog shelters and eventually found an abandoned spaniel.

It was the best thing we could have ever done.

Our home went from stillness to chaos, with a springer spaniel bouncing around it.

During this time, I had failed to notice my period was late. Only when I nearly fainted and kept feeling dizzy did I search out my diary and do period maths. I discovered I was really late and knew I should do a pregnancy test.

It was positive. We both stood staring at the test, tears streaming down our faces.

So the journey for us restarted. Would our fourth pregnancy result in a child for us to raise?

Chapter 4

If we were shocked to find out we were pregnant previously, discovering I was pregnant this time was mind-blowing. I knew the only things doctors can advise are to eat well and avoid stress. I had lived on chicken sandwiches for weeks, as it is hard to eat well when you are sobbing and do not want to go food shopping. So that was a fail next to the 'Eat well' advice.

And we'd just driven to the top of Scotland whilst trying to process years of grief, so that was another big cross next to the 'Stay stress free' advice.

We made an appointment to see my lovely consultant at the clinic. We explained all we had gone through and told him we had then discovered we were pregnant, having probably broken all the rules in the book of how best to avoid a miscarriage.

He was kind, reassuring and caring. He explained that the truth of the matter is however much people try to avoid loss, it is impossible to change a pre-destined outcome. When a baby is meant to survive, they often do. He suggested I had a scan and hopefully that would show us how things were developing.

There on the screen was our baby, growing perfectly, with the loudest heartbeat you ever heard.

Anyone who has lost children in pregnancy will know the fear that grips you in subsequent pregnancies. You get used to feeling scared. Peace feels so removed, and you hover in anxiety, living from appointment to appointment. I was very scared.

Due to my medical history, it was agreed that I would see my consultant every two weeks. Knowing I didn't need to wait months between check-ups did help.

Nausea plagued me as it had in previous pregnancies, along with daily headaches and other symptoms, but they felt a small price to pay. Each scan felt like a milestone and I eventually reached the six-month mark.

Having trained as a counsellor, I was keen to put into practice skills I had taught others, but had never got the chance to use. Pregnancy after a previous loss gives you many opportunities to practise coping strategies and positive reinforcement exercises. Even though I was often plagued with fear, I was able to keep a positive mind frame the majority of the time. But I was seven months pregnant before I allowed myself to imagine bringing home a healthy baby. We knew by this point we were having a little girl and had named her, even though we kept her name a secret. We even prepared her nursery and started to buy clothes.

The pregnancy nausea, which had settled by sixteen weeks, returned in the latter stage of pregnancy, but the countdown to delivery was then on. I knew I had to have a C-section, and this was scheduled for 6th January.

I threw myself into Christmas, knowing this was the perfect distraction, and then it was time to meet our daughter.

The day of the C-section arrived and I am utterly delighted to say that we delivered a healthy baby, and we named her Esme Emilia Promise.

In the weeks that followed, we felt like we were in a bubble of happiness.

We were tired, though, as it turned out we had created a child that did not need sleep. She preferred to stay up all night and nap in the day. I was known for needing a good ten hours of sleep each night, so to go from ten to maybe two was a shock to the system, but not even this could rob me from the joy I was feeling.

We decided from the outset we would never complain about the lack of sleep, that we would view every moment with her as a God-given gift, and I truly believe this helped us get through that sleep deprived period. We chose not to focus on feeling utterly exhausted and ignored the comments from friends and family when they thought we looked like death, as we clearly needed rest.

We never added up the amount of minutes we had had of sleep (notice the minutes there and not hours); we just spoke of the delight and blessing of having her.

You may now be waiting for me to say from three months onwards Esme started to sleep but I am afraid I cannot put that, as she did not sleep until she was four years old. Therefore, from here on in we will not talk about her sleep pattern. Time flew by; children really do grow up so fast.

We adored being parents. It was more than we could ever have hoped it would be. Our resolve to stop at one child was definitely under threat!

By the time Esme turned one, we were also seeing how much she loved being with other children, and the idea of giving her a sibling to grow up with was such a lovely thought.

Finally, a firm decision was made: we wanted another baby, we wanted to give Esme a brother or sister, so the planning began.

Chapter 5

Once we had decided to have another baby, we wanted it to happen instantly. Waiting for anything really tests me.

Thankfully, it only took a few months of trying before we discovered I was pregnant. We were both thrilled.

Weirdly, I was not frightened of losing this baby. I assumed that now we had had Esme, who was born safe and well, our dealings with loss were all behind us. All those familiar pregnancy symptoms came flooding back, and before long, we were back in with the lovely consultant. A scan showed us everything was great and our baby was growing perfectly.

Going for our regular appointments was more relaxed, as we just presumed all would be fine. Esme always came along with us, and we would show her her sibling on the screen and she would listen to the heartbeat.

Time moved pretty fast in this pregnancy, and before we knew it, it was time for our next scan.

We could see our little boy on the screen, but he was really still. Suddenly the atmosphere in the room changed. All that joy and excitement was sucked out, and the mood became sombre.

'Is everything okay, Chris?' I asked.

He just shook his head and said, 'Zoë, I am so sorry. There is no longer a heartbeat.'

I wanted to scream, but I was acutely aware I had a little girl staring at me, whose peace and security rested entirely in my hands. I turned away from her and let tears stream down my face. That silent scream I was now all too familiar with roared within me.

We were asked what we wanted to do; did we want to go the medical route or natural route? This time I did not feel I could make a choice based on how I felt. I wanted to make the decision on what would be best for Esme. I could not imagine her watching me for weeks at home, waiting for labour to start. I was also scared of delivering a dead baby when she was there, and possibly not having a family member free to help us distract her at that crucial moment. I decided to choose the medical option.

It is hard to find the words to tell someone your baby is dead. There is no way of making it easy to say, or hear. It is devastating.

My parents were away on a work trip, so my sister Hayley offered to come and stay, and this was such a gift. We knew she would be able to play with Esme, so we could take time out to grieve together, and she would be able to help when the time came to be admitted into hospital.

We needed to name our baby, so we chose the name Samuel.

A friend found a local consultant who was willing to perform the operation. The consultant was away on holiday, however, so we needed to wait for him to return, but this gave us time to prepare.

Those days of waiting and trying to come to terms with the knowledge that Samuel had died were a nightmare. Each of our losses have shown me first-hand how different grief can be, and how every loss can present its own varying symptoms and feelings. Losing Samuel reinforced this. This grief was dark and heavy and it felt like a weight on my chest. I would often struggle to breathe, and felt I was drowning. This happened regularly after the loss: I felt I was disappearing under the water, where no one could reach me.

I was acutely aware that this time, I was not just grieving for a child I had lost, I was grieving for Esme's brother. I was consumed with fear that she would never have a sibling to play with.

When I finally went to hospital, we were presented with forms to fill in, and asked, 'Would you like his body back, or should we just look after that for you?'

Nothing could have prepared me for that question. I wanted to scream and all I wanted to say was, 'What I want is for my son to be healthy and well, and for me to not be here about to have his body removed from my womb.'

Instead, I quietly asked, 'What do most people do?'

The nurse said most people never have the body back, and the hospital was set up to handle everything. Andy and I had seconds to decide, as she needed to take the forms and process them, so I could be taken to theatre.

Both of us agreed that the least traumatic thing for Esme would be to let the hospital handle things. If we had Samuel's remains, we would then need to arrange a funeral and burial place. So we ticked the box that said 'No'.

As I was being put under in the anaesthetics room, it felt surreal. I was about to deliver my child, while I was unconscious. As I came round in the recovery room I was screaming for my child to be brought back to me.

I felt empty, exhausted and bereft, but was told I could go home.

I also regretted the decision not to have Samuel's body back. We called the hospital that night to ask for the form to be changed but they said it was too late. The moment the form was signed, nothing could be changed.

The days dragged. The physical symptoms of pregnancy did not go. The all-day pregnancy sickness remained and so did the daily headaches. These symptoms tormented me, once again a horrid reminder that I had been pregnant. Now I was not.

My parents returned from their trip and came straight to our house. It was almost like an exact replay of the time when Darcy had died, waiting for them to walk in the door.

It took around six weeks for the pregnancy symptoms to go. Soon after my monthly cycle resumed and slowly my body started to recover from the pregnancy, the loss and the operation.

We did not know how long we should wait following loss before we tried again but the consultant told us as long as we had one normal period before trying, that would be fine. As soon as that happened, we agreed to try for another baby. We were blessed to get pregnant quickly.

We decided to tell our immediate family at our Christmas Eve party.

Esme, Andy and I all shouted simultaneously, 'We are having a baby!'

Everyone was thrilled, hugs were exchanged and Esme did a happy dance.

One of my least favourite pregnancy symptoms then chose to present itself, with a sudden need to go to the bathroom. I ran to the loo. And discovered I had started to bleed.

Chapter 6

I did not know what to do. I shouted for Andy and I told him what had happened. We hugged until I felt calmer, and I asked him to tell people and make sure Esme was kept happy at all times, then to send my mum and sister up to me.

They came upstairs and we tried to think of positive things to hold onto. It is hard to think up hopeful things to say once someone has previously lost four babies, but we did our best.

I rejoined the party, and made a firm decision that whatever happened with the pregnancy over the following few days, I would focus on Esme. We would make sure she had the best Christmas ever and deal with everything else privately.

The bleeding continued. It never became heavy, but it was a constant reminder that yet again I was losing a baby. I discussed it with a GP and he told me I had definitely miscarried, but since it was fairly early on in the pregnancy, a scan was not needed for confirmation.

I think I deserve an Oscar for getting through that Christmas period, pretending things were fine. I smiled, laughed and ensured Esme had the time of her life. Post New Year, the bleeding stopped, but a full-blown period never showed up. I started to feel sicker and sicker. I had now been pregnant six times. I knew pregnancy symptoms like the back of my hand but this was so severe I was struggling even to speak because of the nausea. At Esme's second birthday party, I sat on the sofa, praying no one would speak to me.

Joining in her party games was torture. I became a master at descriptive hand gestures so I could avoid opening my mouth, which often resulted in me vomiting.

We decided whatever the GP had said, a scan was vital, so we booked one. We were not expecting good news—we had already accepted that the baby had been lost. This was more to find out what was wrong, and why I was so ill.

The scan was performed, and to our surprise, there was a baby. The scanning equipment the doctor was using was very dated so nothing was clear, but what we knew for sure was I had not miscarried, and I was still pregnant.

We decided to travel to see my normal consultant who had become a trusted friend. We thought it best to leave it a few weeks for the next scan as we wanted, the next time we saw the baby, for things to be clear-cut.

Two weeks went by in a blur of sickness and nausea. If I thought I had experienced severe pregnancy sickness before, nothing compared to this. It was there twenty-four hours a day. I did not even get a reprieve through the night as I often woke up to vomit.

The day arrived for my scan and there on the screen was not one baby but two!

We sat there open-mouthed.

Chris said he would not be surprised if we lost one of the babies, as it was clear to see one of the twins was much bigger than the other. In his experience he said this could often mean one of the babies would not make it, but only time would tell.

It was odd: knowing one of the twins was less likely to survive meant we could not celebrate the fact we were having twins at all. Even telling people that we were having two babies felt sad, as we had to make it clear that both probably would not make it. Because of this, we only told close family and a few friends, and then just waited for our next scan.

The nausea and sickness continued but I also started to get other symptoms which were not normal. I knew something was going wrong with me and my body was struggling.

One Saturday evening, I told Andy I could not cope any more. I felt so ill I thought I might die. I could hardly move, was non-stop vomiting, and had severe pains just under my ribs. We called the GP and was told to go to the emergency clinic where a doctor would see me.

When we arrived, a male nurse practitioner was on duty. He took one look at me and said, 'You need to be in hospital.' He believed the symptoms were liver-related.

It was agreed I would be admitted into hospital under the care of a liver specialist. I was scared, both for my health and any effect it might have on my babies.

Tests were arranged. Scans showed my gallbladder had completely failed and was full of stones. The liver specialist did not want to operate until the babies were born, which meant I would have to remain like that for months. My obstetrician stepped in and said leaving me in that state was not an option. He doubted whether the babies or I would survive if the surgery was not done as quickly as possible.

Weeks of in-house medical discussions were held. We had even started looking for other specialists who might take over my care, as it was clear to us my gallbladder needed removing as soon as possible, not only for my sake but also for the survival of our children. I was now bedridden, constantly vomiting and in utter agony twenty-four hours a day. I could not even lie completely flat as my insides felt stuck together.

I had to go for my next baby scan and check-up and I dragged myself to the clinic. There we discovered one of the twins had died. I was now only carrying one healthy baby.

We did not have time to grieve: we had to choose to focus on this one little fighter, and get me better. We were very aware of the risk to the baby and to myself. One of us might not survive.

We finally got the green light from the consultant, and he agreed to do the operation. After some preparation, the gallbladder removal operation was booked. I was told they would not be able to monitor the health of the remaining baby while I was under general anaesthetic, but that babies usually coped well.

As he left the room, I sobbed and sobbed in Andy's arms. The thought of this baby also going under a general anaesthetic was terrifying. We knew, however, it was the only way to save their life and mine and therefore we had no other option. I prayed and asked God to protect us both.

What should have been a straightforward operation quickly proved to be far from that.

When removing my gallbladder, they found it was so infected it had adhered to my liver. It took them hours to safely complete the operation but it was deemed a success.

That night was a blur of agony and morphine. They could not tell me if my baby had survived, as they did not have the right scanner at the hospital.

The next day I decided I wanted to go home, and they agreed. We arranged a scan on the way home and thankfully it showed the baby was fine.

The next couple of weeks were terrible. I did not feel like I was getting better. The pain I had previously had was still there, I was still vomiting and still bedridden.

My GP said she wanted my liver and bile ducts rescanned. We could tell from the scan specialist's face that something was wrong when the scan was being conducted.

The consultant informed us that the position of my gallstones had changed since the scan prior to my surgery. One of the stones had left the gallbladder, and had been missed during surgery, that stone was now stuck in my bile duct. To get it out would mean accessing it via my back, which would be dangerous and complicated, particularly because of my pregnancy.

The appointment ended with him agreeing to speak to other expert colleagues, so a course of action could be agreed upon.

Days later we were informed that my specialist definitely would not perform the operation as he felt it was far too dangerous, but it was determined that it did have to be done, as I was still so sick. Another liver specialist also refused to take on the operation, as the risks were far too high. He told Andy on the phone that I might die if I didn't have the operation—but I may also die if I did. It was a no-win situation.

My best hope still—for our baby and I—was to have the surgery.

Andy begged him to save my life. He asked him to imagine if I was his wife—wouldn't he want someone to help her? By the end of the phone call, the consultant had agreed to take on the surgery.

That evening our home was full of crying people, my parents and us. Every time I looked at Esme, I cried more. It seemed a real possibility I would never see her grow up.

We felt helpless but knew there was one thing we could do. We could pray—a lot.

Mum and Andy called every contact they had around the UK and asked them to start praying.

The next morning, we headed to the hospital to have the scan that was needed before surgery.

All I could do was pray for a miracle, that the stone would be gone and no surgery would be needed. We had been told that the stone was too big to pass naturally. I knew God had not healed me so far, but I truly believed it was possible.

When the doctor finally rang, he said, 'You won't believe this but the stone has gone. There are no stones in your bile ducts at all!'

No surgery would be needed.

I remained in shock for the following weeks, but my health started to return. I continued being sick, but the pain had gone and strength was starting to return to my body. I was no longer bedridden and it felt like we had turned a massive corner. I finally knew I was going to survive and so was the daughter I was carrying.

We only had a few weeks of peace before another scare reared its head.

It took three weeks before we knew everything was fine.

The stress of everything we had been through was enormous.

We crawled our way to our thirty-sixth week of pregnancy.

During a scan, my consultant thought the baby was a little too small, so I constantly prayed that she would put on weight and asked God to make her weigh 6lb 6oz.

Then out of the blue—five days before my C-section date—I started to itch.

My whole body was *violently* itchy. Every limb, every part of my body, inside my eyes, under my nail beds, everywhere. Within hours, I had open wounds on my legs where I had scratched in my sleep. The only thing that brought a tiny bit of relief was bags of ice all over my body.

We called my covering consultant and he told me to go to the local hospital. They would check the baby, and do a blood test to see if I had developed a pregnancy condition which affects the liver, called obstetric cholestasis (OC).

On the Friday, the doctor told me I did have OC, and I had it severely. He said he would like the baby to be delivered urgently. My covering consultant agreed that the baby should be delivered within the next twenty-four hours.

Before long we were walking to theatre. Scared. Itchy. Expectant.

Within minutes, we were being asked if we were ready to meet our baby girl. The curtain was pulled down and out she popped, screaming away.

Tears of relief and joy flowed, as I hugged my precious little girl.

The nurse then took her to the scales to be weighed.

Everyone started guessing at her weight. Even the consultants were throwing in their guesses … and the nurse shouted out, 'She weighs 6lbs 6oz.'

At that, I burst into tears yet again.

We had done it, we had finished the race and here we were with our two little girls, feeling utterly blessed.

When Bronte Jemima Hope was safely in our arms, we felt able to grieve for her twin we had sadly lost. Knowing there should have been two little girls in the crooks of my arms hurt, and it hurt a lot.

We had named Bronte's twin sister Isabella. The thought of never seeing both Bronte and Isabella side by side in a cot was so painful, but this grief never removed an ounce of the joy we felt having Bronte in our arms.

We felt so blessed to have two children to raise.

When Bronte reached six months old, I decided we needed to do something to help others who had gone through loss. I spent weeks looking at what would have helped us in our darkest hour, and that is when the idea of 'Saying Goodbye' was born.

Chapter 7

I knew we needed to turn our pain into something positive. I simply refused to accept that our losses, our tears and our children's lives would have no legacy. I look on the bright side, and believe that if you have been through something, you are now the best equipped to help others. With all of this firmly in mind I started to consider what we had most needed when going through our darkest hours of grief. What had we hoped to find?

It then hit me! What the country needed was a national service where everyone could honour their children and formally say goodbye to them. We had seen online that there were small services arranged in hospitals or chapels, but they weren't coordinated, so it was hard for anyone to know what to expect when they attended one.

There was also a lack of organisations run by people who had suffered loss first-hand. We knew from our experiences that there was a clear divide in support dependent on what stage you lost your baby. We were made to feel that the babies we lost early in pregnancy were less significant than those who were lost later. We could not disagree more. Every baby matters, no matter how long they live. They were loved and deserved to be acknowledged.

We had identified something missing, in the UK and globally, and I felt very strongly that Andy and I could provide it.

It would have been quite easy at this stage to feel overwhelmed, but we honestly did not. We felt equipped with both our corporate background and my past counselling training. In addition, we had experienced loss and had walked that agonising journey; nothing could have trained us better than that.

As it happened, we ran a global event, PR and marketing organisation, and we knew that we could turn our company's expertise into charitable work. We decided that we would launch a not-for-profit division of our company, dedicated to helping bereaved parents, and we would name it 'Saying Goodbye'. We did not know how we would fit it all in time-wise, but we were determined to try!

The first major task was to plan our remembrance service.

We knew this service needed to be special.

We did not want to recreate anything that was already out there—it was important to create something that was currently missing.

We looked at what we would want in a service. These were the five crucial things:

1. We would want the service in a beautiful historic building, not in a hospital or a hidden chapel. We would want the venue itself to scream out the importance of our cherished children, who had very little time to make their imprint on this world.

2. We would want the service to be for everyone. Not just for parents who had lost, but also for their parents, siblings, grandparents, aunts, uncles. Even friends should be welcome to attend, recognising

that grief touches so many more people than just the grieving parents.

3. We would want the service to welcome anyone who had lost recently or historically. We were acutely aware that if there was a lack of support for those who suffered loss today, fifty to seventy years ago, there was no support at all. It was crucially important to offer everyone the time and opportunity to grieve.

4. We would want the service to be for anyone of any faith, or none. This could be done by including both traditional funeral elements, which are often Christian-based, and secular elements, such as music and poetry.

5. We would want the service to be for anyone who had lost a baby in pregnancy, at birth or in early years, as this would show the world that gestation is not relevant when it comes to loss.

The list was drawn up and we decided the perfect venues would be cathedrals. They offered us everything we could ask for and more. They were both beautiful and historic, and they met the need for a venue that welcomed both Christian and secular events. Cathedrals are used for royal events and momentous occasions, so this would also reinforce our message to the wider community and media that *every baby lost matters.*

We started to approach cathedrals, and they thankfully gave a resounding 'yes' to holding the services there. As our event management company would be the organisers and planners, cathedrals were willing to agree to a service. They knew we had solid experience of planning high quality events and were qualified and insured. This was a great hurdle to leap. Secondly, as Andy and

I were speaking with personal experience, they saw that we could deliver a meaningful and important service to families dealing with baby loss.

Now we could have just arranged one service and seen how that had gone, but if we were going to do this, we needed to do it well, and ideally that meant launching nationally. So we arranged seven Saying Goodbye services, including events at St Paul's Cathedral, London, York Minster and St Mary's Cathedral, Edinburgh. The bar was set high, and we were determined to exceed all expectations.

The next crucial task was to invite ambassadors to champion the cause. We discussed who would be appropriate. We were aware that we needed a mix of highly respected medical people with a public profile, and other media stars who would support the cause. We wrote a list of dream people, and started to reach out to each of them. Virtually every person agreed. Within weeks, we had a wonderful team of high profile ambassadors including Professor Lord Winston, Nigella Lawson and Gabby Logan.

Thanks to our PR backgrounds, we knew we needed to get the word out, and we were able to call upon all our media friends and acquaintances, and ask for their help in promoting the services.

The first big article went to press, and that is when things exploded for us. It was the first time I realised how exposed we were going to be. It was one thing saying we were happy to share our story to help others, but now we were putting that into practice.

Our personal—and until then very private—story of loss was splashed over a national newspaper, and anyone who cared to read it could. We believed it would remain a UK feature, but that paper sold the story to various media outlets around the world. A quick Google search showed us our journey of loss was now in papers in New York, Japan and elsewhere.

Many people that weekend asked us what it felt like seeing our pain written in black and white in a broadsheet, and the only way I could describe it was it felt like we were walking down the street naked. I felt so vulnerable and it was incredibly hard for me. It took a whole week for me to feel pleased we had done the feature. Gradually that feeling of being over-exposed passed, and it was replaced with a feeling of relief that we had done what was needed.

Within a couple of weeks of the article going to press and the first service being advertised, we were inundated with people wanting information and support.

The workload was immense but, bit by bit, we could see that something very special was emerging.

Before we knew it, our first Saying Goodbye service (at Exeter Cathedral) was upon us. BBC Radio 4's *Woman's Hour* asked if they could attend and record the service, as well as interview us. Of course, we said 'yes', but that certainly added to the nerves on the big day.

On the day, the team arrived at the cathedral. Everything we had planned and prepared over the previous months was about to become a reality.

The journalist arrived and started interviewing Andy and I, and one of the team, on our personal experiences of loss. Meanwhile others were manically setting up the cathedral.

As we stood in the cathedral waiting for people to arrive we were petrified, but as soon as the first person arrived, peace came upon me. As we were building Saying Goodbye, we had decided the most important thing for us was to always focus on the individual and never on the masses. We said that whatever we did, we needed to be prepared to do it for just one family, and if we helped more, that was a bonus. Therefore, as soon as that first seat was filled, our mission was complete: we knew one heart could be helped that day.

Person after person then entered the nave, and we watched as women, men and children filled seats. People of every age were sitting alongside each other, all with the same desire to honour a baby that had been lost.

The service was utterly beautiful. We had carefully designed the order of service to be a mix of secular music, poems, stories of hope and two acts of remembrance.

The first act was traditional, as we wanted people to feel comfortable and at ease, so we had chosen candle lighting. Seeing people stand in line down the cathedral, waiting for their turn to light those candles was quite a moment. For the first time, I saw the faces of the people we were helping. You could see the pain etched on their faces, but you could also see their gratitude for this opportunity to stand alongside others who just got it.

The second act of remembrance was hand-bell ringing. When I had come up with this idea and approached the team at Exeter Cathedral about it, they had looked at me as if I was mad. It took them a few weeks to accept that it was a good idea, and it was agreed that it would form a pinnacle point in the service. I just prayed it would work.

We struggled to get hold of a set of traditional hand-bells that could be passed around the cathedral (it turned out hand-bells are very expensive and should only be handled in certain ways) but eventually a local hand-bell group volunteered their bells for the occasion.

When the big moment arrived, the choir stood and started singing the most wonderful anthem, and the team started to pass the hand-bells down the rows of seats. All through the cathedral, you could hear the sound of bells, and every chime represented a baby that had been lost. Some families rang those bells more than ten times, others just once, but every chime was giving their baby a sound, and all could hear it. As the bells were chiming inside, we rang the main cathedral bells, so all around the city people could hear ringing. It was one of the most powerful and beautiful moments of my life.

The service was a resounding success. People had come from near and far to attend (one couple had even flown in from Holland just to attend, and another woman from America). We knew this was the start of something great.

The *Woman's Hour* broadcast managed to capture the true spirit of the occasion and the stories of the people who shared. In fact, we could not have been happier with the piece they kindly produced and aired, it was perfect.

To show you how these services can impact lives, here is a portion of a letter we received from a service guest.

Dear Saying Goodbye,

My boyfriend and I first started trying for a baby 12 years ago. After a year or so of nothing happening, we were referred to the hospital and were prescribed with fertility drugs to help kick-start our attempts.

We were delighted, after the second cycle of drugs, to be pregnant.

Within days of our positive pregnancy test, we were utterly desperate when I started to miscarry—there were no words to describe how we felt when the loss of our baby was confirmed and the next few months were a real period of grief.

Friends and family at the time were sympathetic and reassuring and we were overjoyed to be pregnant again within six months.

At around eight weeks, I again miscarried and this became the pattern of our lives over the next ten years.

All in all, we lost 14 babies, our final attempt culminating in an ectopic pregnancy with emergency surgery where I almost lost my life. At this point, we finally decided to stop our journey to have a baby.

Countless investigations, referrals, tests, and treatments failed to find any reasons why we could not hold onto our babies and the only treatment I was given to help mend my broken mind and heart was Prozac.

Our losses became a source of discomfort for the majority of our friends and family. They moved from the 'at least you know you can get pregnant' and 'so and so lost their baby and now they have three' to just ignoring the situation or feeling dreadfully embarrassed when they had to tell us that they were pregnant or they were doing fun things with their family.

We started to not tell people when we became pregnant or had another loss, as it was too difficult to have the conversation and feel their awkwardness. It was not that they did not love us or feel for us it was that there was nothing they could say or do that would make it better.

I first heard of Saying Goodbye through our local paper advertising an upcoming service.

I remember reading the article and, for a few days, I thought of nothing else.

I had buried my losses deep within my heart and had tried to shut out my emotions so that I could function in my normal life. The idea of having special time to remember and honour my children was a real revelation, but I was worried that if I went, I would open a wound I would not be able to close.

At this stage in our lives, we had started the adoption process and had been provisionally linked to a six-month-old. I was torn between recognising my longed-for birth children and not wanting to restart the grieving process.

I still was not sure on the day of the service, but something inside told me I should go, and I nervously went and found a seat.

I can honestly say that I will never regret my decision.

The Saying Goodbye service gave me the time and space to formally recognise all of my babies and the experience of being with people who just knew how it felt was a real strength. The loss of a baby by miscarriage is never formally recognised by ceremony—no funeral service is held, no date is noted, no names are recorded. As I stood with other parents and proudly rang the bell for my 14 babies, I felt unbearable sadness but also a great privilege in being able to properly celebrate their existence.

For the first time ever I felt my tears of grief, loss and love were allowed, shared and understood.

Later as I made my way back to the car park I saw another couple that had been sitting a few aisles over from me. We both got to the ticket machine at the same time and with no words, we hugged each other. It was such a powerful moment that will stay with me for ever—a shared understanding.

I am writing this now as my one-year-old daughter sleeps up-stairs.

Life has moved on as it does, and it is really good.

Saying Goodbye has really helped that process. I was able to properly recognise my children, and, whilst they will never be forgotten, move on in my life with the knowledge that I'm not alone and that there are others who truly understand.

Thanks, Helen[1]

Immediately after the first service, we realised that we needed to widen the support we were offering. It was not enough to just offer remembrance services, we needed to offer full emotional support and also campaign for change in how care is provided nationally. We were acutely aware of how much work this would be, but it was needed, and we were determined to rise to the challenge.

---

1   Used with permission

It was roughly around this time that we started to see that what was supposed to have been a 'not-for-profit division of a company' was quickly becoming more like a stand-alone organisation. In fact, within six weeks of launching we were forging ahead as one of the leading support organisations for baby loss in the UK and we were being encouraged to apply for charitable status.

We decided to name the registered charity 'The Mariposa Trust' (*mariposa* is Spanish for 'butterfly'), and the Saying Goodbye brand we had developed would become the leading support division of The Mariposa Trust.

Practically overnight this small not-for-profit division of our company had become a massive organisation in its own right, but of course it had no money at all!

At this stage, we were unwilling to take donations from anyone, as we wanted to prove the charity's worth to the general public. So our company put in every penny it had and we personally re-mortgaged our home and emptied every bank account we had (including our pension) to ensure the work could continue.

We then had to make a colossal decision about our company. For Saying Goodbye and The Mariposa Trust to keep going it would need the company to provide all of its time to the charity. This would mean letting go of all our major clients and event portfolio, which had been built over a thirteen-year period. We knew it was something we had to do, as by now thousands of people were being helped each month.

Therefore, our small not-for-profit division became a registered charity and our company became its supplier. It is quite easy to write this but it is pretty impossible to write what a gigantic decision this was, and how monumental it was for Andy and myself, and of course for our entire family. Everything we had built for the past thirteen years was being given to the charity. Most of our family and friends thought we were mad, but they all supported us and we were so grateful.

The first seven services were a massive success, and the charity continued to grow and develop. So many hearts were touched, and we had begun to develop a great reputation for offering national support to people. There were so many people we had supported who wanted to give back to the charity, so they became volunteers, and our team started to grow, filled with amazing talented people.

Before long The Mariposa Trust started to develop other divisions to work alongside the primary division, Saying Goodbye. 'GrowingYou' was the first to be launched, which offers support to those who are pregnant following the loss of a baby. We saw how desperately this was needed, as so many people the charity was supporting were getting pregnant again quickly, and they were begging us to walk that journey with them, so it was a very natural development for us.

Here is the statement Lord Winston released:

Miscarriage and stillbirth is often something that's not acknowledged or talked about in the UK, and people certainly do not appreciate how utterly distressing it is for parents, and indeed their extended families. It is a loss of a precious life, and whether the loss happens in early or late pregnancy, at birth or in infancy, it is traumatic, and a natural grief process must be allowed to happen. Sadly, a lot of doctors and nurses see loss on such a regular basis, the right support and follow-up advice is just not offered, which results in the vast amount of parents never coming to terms with losing their baby, and sadly they are not able to move forward with their lives as they become stuck in a cycle of grief.

I am delighted to be an ambassador for a ground-breaking charity called The Mariposa Trust. They have two divisions, Saying Goodbye and GrowingYou. Saying Goodbye offers support and befriending to anyone who has lost a baby, and it also runs national remembrance services, which allow families to come together to mourn their babies. The services are held at cathedrals across the UK, and more information can be found at www.sayinggoodbye. org. GrowingYou offers support to anyone who is pregnant following loss, as the fear of losing again can be profound for many people—www.growingyou.org

The charity was founded by Zoë and Andrew Clark-Coates, who themselves have lost five babies. Having experienced this agonising pain and grief themselves, they are perfectly qualified to not only offer wonderful support, but also to be a voice in the national media and at governmental level.

I am so proud to be working with The Mariposa Trust, the services and support the charity offers is groundbreaking, and because of its work, we have seen a change in the nation, as people are becoming more aware of the scale of baby loss, and the support that is needed. Miscarriage and stillbirth has also become more widely understood, and families now know that their pain and loss has been heard and recognised.

The Mariposa Trust then launched 'Holding Hope' and 'Waiting for You'. 'Holding Hope' supports people who are considering or are receiving fertility treatment. 'Waiting for You' befriends those on the path to adoption. Most of the people supported in this division have lost a baby in the past, but they have then chosen to have a family, or expand their existing family by adopting.

The final two divisions are relatively new. These are 'Love in Every Tear' and 'So Cherished'. 'Love in Every Tear' supports family members and friends who are also grieving for the loss of a child, but its primary function is to help them support others through loss. The public were begging us to help them support their friends or loved ones, as it is so hard to know what to say, or how to best offer support to the bereaved, so we knew this division was vital. 'So Cherished' was also then launched due to public demand. Sadly, many parents are given the terrible news that their baby will die at birth or shortly after due to illness or genetic issues. Whilst we could have supported these people through the Saying Goodbye division, we recognised that this is a unique situation, and people needed specialised support and befriending.

As you can imagine a huge amount has happened in the last four years.

The charity's support now reaches in excess of 50,000 people each week, and the website has over 650,000 hits every month. It has a social media presence that can reach up to two million people in twenty-four hours, and that figure still astounds me. The team is made up of over 240 amazing volunteers, who work on various divisions and projects, from fundraising to hospital development, and from the PR team to befriending.

The charity has held grand balls at the Savoy Hotel, London and a private reception at 10 Downing Street. It has been made a stakeholder partner with the Department of Health and has become a leading voice in the media. It has launched across the whole of the United States of America and Canada and into mainland Europe.

If you had asked us on day one of launching Saying Goodbye if this is what our lives would look like we would have probably laughed. Nothing could have prepared us for the extent of the need that was clearly lacking in this area of loss. I would have never dreamt that we could be helping the amount of people we are now.

However, that is how life should be. Life is unpredictable and if we commit to living it passionately and authentically, amazing things can happen.

We are so excited to see what the next ten years will look like—and the years after that too! If you would like support from The Mariposa Trust, or would like to help the charity in some way, please get in touch.

www.mariposatrust.org

www.sayinggoodbye.org

Daily Support

When I was first asked to write a book, I considered what sort of book I needed when going through loss.

I had needed two things: personal stories I could relate to, and something I could pick up daily to give me support. It was obvious this was the book I should write.

It is always hard to know how much information to share when you tell your story, how much information is too much? If you do not share enough it is pointless, as it will help no one. It is with this in mind I have shared my story and I hope by pouring out my heart on these pages, you have been helped.

The next part of the book is the daily support section. It was hard to decide how many days I should include. Thirty days was definitely not enough. Sixty would have been acceptable, but ninety felt just right. You may want to read multiple days in one sitting, you may want to read the whole lot in one go, or you may prefer to read it as I wrote it, which is one page for each day. I want you to feel I am walking with you as your heart starts to heal, and I would love for you to see this book and me as a friend.

My hope and my wish for you is that you will soon start to see the sun rising again, and colour will refill your life.

Much love,

Zoë x

Day 1

Nothing can prepare you for the shock when you hear the news that your baby has died. It feels like one second you are in a brightly lit garden, flowers blooming, sun shining, and the next moment a trap door opens beneath you and you are plunged into darkness. One minute you are thinking of baby names and planning your future, the next you feel like you have no future at all, as the world seems bleak and hopeless.

I think to truly understand the pain you have to have experienced it too. It is pretty impossible to describe and definitely impossible to imagine. And this is exactly why you cannot prepare for losing a baby. Whatever stats are thrown at you, however much you are told 'Don't get too excited until you pass twelve weeks just in case', when you discover you are pregnant, dreams are instantly born, and when they are snatched from you, hearts shatter.

TASK FOR THE DAY:

Sit, reflect and allow yourself to cry.
There is healing in the weeping.

Some days—in fact,
on a lot of days—you may
doubt you can survive this
pain, this grief that's
drowning you.
Let me reassure you,
you can survive
and you will survive.

Zoë Clark-Coates

Day 2

Did you know every child a woman carries actually changes their DNA? Science has now shown that cells of every child remain in the mother's body, whether the baby died in the womb, or was born healthy and well. I find this so comforting and I hope you do too.

When you lose a baby you can feel empty, and even beginning to accept your child has gone forever is agonising. To know part of them remains within you (or your partner) can be such a gift as you can make their legacy live on.

TASK FOR THE DAY:

If you never saw your child—imagine what your child would have looked like.

If you did see your child—imagine what they would have looked like as they grew older.

Your baby may have not lived for long but they were a person, a cherished person, and one of the terribly hard things to accept is that you will never get to see their face mature. Imagining what they would have looked like and putting a face to the grief can help you move forward.

Your child that never saw
life outside of the womb
has now changed the
core of you.

Your DNA will simply
never be the same.

Zoë Clark-Coates

Day 3

Do not panic if you run out of tears. Sometimes you may become emotionally barren. You may have cried endlessly, you may have screamed, shouted, and asked 'why?' countless times but then, all of a sudden, nothing! You feel numb, frozen and wonder what has happened.

Does this mean I do not care anymore? Does this mean I have had a breakdown? Does this mean my baby does not matter? All these are common questions and the answer to each is highly likely to be no. As humans, we have a limit to the capacity we can cope with. Our brains can only process so much trauma, and that is why we can have periods of just feeling numb and cut off from reality. Do not fight it and do not worry, just keep talking about your loss and eventually you will find yourself peeling off another layer of the grief onion.

TASK FOR THE DAY:

Find two pieces of music you really like and listen to them both.
During each piece of music do not think of anything, just breathe deeply.

Often I ran out of tears.
I sat there numb.
Is there a word that
explains this state of
being? 'Broken' is the
only word I can find.

Zoë Clark-Coates

Day 4

Be patient. If you are anything like me, patience is not something that comes naturally to you, and even if you are blessed with this gift of being able to sit and wait, grief can be the ultimate test of it.

Grieving is a long process. For some it is a journey of a lifetime, for others the rawest part of grief may be processed in a matter of weeks or months, but no one has an ability to skip the process or speed it up, all one can do is face it a day at a time.

I certainly got frustrated on many occasions, and I actually remember saying 'I am bored of crying', 'I am fed up of feeling an emotional wreck', and I hankered for the time when I felt happy and at peace. However, I want to assure you if you stick with it, if you allow yourself to move through the stepping stones of grief, you will find yourself on the other side of that river, or at least in a boat in which you can safely sail.

TASK FOR THE DAY:

Find a poem or write a poem that best sums up your experience of grief.

GRIEVING FOR SOMEONE IS

THE ULTIMATE ACT OF LOVE,

AND IT IS CERTAINLY NOT AN ACT

WE CAN CHOOSE TO SKIP BY.

Zoë Clark-Coates

Day 5

Feeling tired and exhausted is one hundred percent normal. The shock, the trauma, the hundreds of questions and thoughts that run through your mind every single day, as your brain tries to accept and process what has just happened to you can quickly manifest in feelings of utter exhaustion. You may even find it hard to get out of bed, and cooking a meal can feel like an epic task. My advice is to rest as much as possible. Just as you would rest following the flu to allow your body to heal, you also need time for your body to recover following shock and trauma. My one tip is to try to get out of the house at least once each day—even if it is for a walk around the garden, or around your neighbourhood. Staring at the same four walls day in, day out can also be tough, and it is good to not totally disconnect from the world.

TASK FOR THE DAY:

Do something special for you ... look after you. Whether that be a long hot bath, or ordering your favourite takeaway food, or simply going for a walk.

When you have gone through loss, you can quickly forget or not even care about looking after yourself, life just becomes about survival, and it is good to stop for a moment and do something nice for you.

Is it normal to feel tired—
exhausted even—following loss?
Yes, totally normal.

Your brain is trying to process
and come to terms with the
gravity of your situation, and this
takes a huge amount of energy.
Rest as much as possible, and
sleep when you can.

Zoë Clark-Coates

Day 6

The weight of grief is huge. Until I had gone through baby loss, I had no clue how consuming grief could be. Yes, I had lost family members and friends, but grieving for them was so different. In that grief, I was able to continue with life and the waves of grief were not all-consuming for days on end. When you lose a child that you have created your heart shatters, and the grief is indescribable for many people. For a long time after a loss, it can be hard to see a light at the end of the tunnel and because of that, each day can feel endless.

What helped me in these weeks and months was to keep reading other people's stories, of how they had survived loss. I would also constantly remind myself that it might feel hopeless right now but one day it will feel very different. If you can grasp this and hold onto it, it can help prevent grief slipping into depression.

Task for the day:

Write a letter to yourself five years in the future.

Tell yourself how you hope life will now be and the lessons you hope you will have learned. This is such a good exercise as it can help you see past the now and helps you look into a positive future. Five years from now, you can open it and see what you wrote.

I wanted someone, anyone,
to rescue me. The agony I felt,
and the sheer weight of the grief
I was carrying, made me feel like
I was suffocating. I quickly
discovered no one could swoop
in and free me from the journey
of grief. I just had to dress for
battle and move through each
day, trusting I would survive.

Zoë Clark-Coates

Day 7

Friends that 'get it' can be such a blessing when going through loss and even friends that don't can offer you support. If you are anything like me, you love to feel self-sufficient and struggle to admit that you may need help, but I beg you to open up to people you can trust. It is so tempting to put on a brave face, a fake smile and pretend you are fine, but friends want the real you. By opening up you give them the chance to offer you true compassion and empathy and this can make your friendship even stronger.

If your friend were going through something terrible, would you want them to talk with you? Would you want them to reach out and ask for support? I am sure the answer is 'yes', and if it is, that means you need to offer them that chance to be a great friend to you. Talk to them! Admit it when you are struggling! Say yes to help!

TASK FOR THE DAY:

Call a friend and have a proper chat … a real chat.
Do not just say all is fine; talk about the pain you are experiencing.

Volunteer some hours.
Focus on something
outside yourself. Devote
a slice of your energies
towards making the world
suck less every week.

Shonda Rhimes

Day 8

Some days you may want to be surrounded by people and other days you may just want to be alone, both feelings are fine. Some people fear being on their own post loss, others crave it. No feeling you feel is wrong, and it is very normal to feel a host of contradictory feelings all in the space of a few hours.

Being alone can be helpful at times, it gives you time and space to just be you. I encourage everyone to take a little time each day to just think, to just be. For some it may be possible to have an hour in the day to sit and reflect, for others you may only have the time it takes for you to shower. But however much time you have, use it to be real. If you need to cry, cry! If you need to scream, scream! If you want to watch a stand-up comic and laugh, laugh! Do what feels right for you.

TASK FOR THE DAY:

Take the time to do something you feel you need to do. So if that means you need a good cry, do that.

If you want to escape from thinking, maybe put on a film.

The important thing is to offer yourself the space to do what you want to do.

Sometimes,
you may just
want to be alone,
and that's okay.

Zoë Clark-Coates

Day 9

When life and circumstances make people feel out of control, their brains can freak out and before they know it, they are obsessing over the oddest things. It could be over how clean the house is, how people are behaving … anything. If this happens to you, be aware that this is probably just your way of trying to feel more in control. Nothing makes you feel more out of control than grief, and it is one hundred percent normal to want to feel secure and stable again.

TASK FOR THE DAY:

Look at your behaviour and things you have been doing. Are you doing anything different to normal?

How does it make you feel when you do those things?

Does doing certain things help you?

Grief can make you completely
obsess about tiny, seemingly
irrelevant, things.
This is your brain's way of trying
to take back some control,
as nothing makes you feel as
utterly powerless as grief.

Zoë Clark-Coates

Day 10

I had never seen so many pregnancy bumps, prams and babies in the weeks that followed our losses. It seemed overnight everyone was pregnant. People also started asking me, 'Do you have children?' and each time it felt like a thump to my stomach. With hindsight, I realise that those bumps, babies and prams had been there before but I failed to notice them. People had probably always asked me about children, too, but because I was not in grief, I would just answer without a thought and it never left a mark on me, but at the time, it felt like I had a flashing light over my head.

I wish I could tell you here how to stop it from hurting, but I am afraid I cannot. When you see something in front of you that you so desperately want, of course it will hurt, but I can assure you the pain gets less over time. I can also tell you how I coped with it. I made a choice that whenever I saw someone who was pregnant I would choose to feel happy for them and see them as walking messages of hope. They were pregnant, or they were holding a baby, that meant it was possible to have a happy ending. By making this choice, it really helped me, and in time, the pain went, and I felt joy when I saw people living my dream.

Task for the day:

Try to accept it is okay to feel bad when you see something that hurts you, and realise this in no way makes you a bad person; it just makes you human.

IN THE MONTHS FOLLOWING OUR
LOSSES, I SAW MORE PRAMS,
MORE BABIES, AND MORE BABY
BUMPS THAN EVER BEFORE; I
GUESS YOUR EYES ARE ALWAYS
DRAWN TO THE THINGS YOU SO
DESPERATELY WANT.

Zoë Clark-Coates

Day 11

When we lose a baby, we are robbed of so many memories and of so many experiences with that child. We can only imagine their first Christmas and their first day at school and this is probably one of the hardest things to accept. It is so hard to have very few or no memories at all with your child outside the womb and for Andy and I this was hard to explain to people.

Task for the day:

Write a letter to the baby you lost. Tell them how much you love them; explain the plans, hopes and dreams you had for their life.

If you planned to do certain things with them, or places you would take them, write it all in this letter.

This is your chance to put your heart and soul into words.

Be warned this can be an incredibly painful experience, but also know it can be truly healing. Ensure you give yourself the time and space to do this exercise and do not do it just before going to an important meeting. I always advise people to give themselves a good three to four hours to write a letter like this and then ensure you have an evening to recover, as you may feel emotionally drained afterwards.

What should you then do with the letter? Well, some people treasure it forever; others bury it with their child. Some burn it and as they see the smoke rise, they feel it is going to their baby. Do whatever you feel is right—remember: you set the rules—no one else!

When you do a pregnancy test and it
is positive, you are not just a mother
while it stays positive, you remain a
mother forever. The two lines mean
your DNA has literally changed and
whether your baby lives or dies, you
will be their parent for eternity.

Zoë Clark-Coates

Day 12

It is kind of shocking when your world falls to pieces, and everything and everyone around you carries on with life. How can the birds continue to sing? How can people carry on loving life? It is like you have become frozen in time and are now watching life like a movie. As the weeks and months roll by, life becomes more real again, but you will never forget that point in time when life stood still.

TASK FOR THE DAY:

Try to accept you are not alone and that people do understand the pain you are experiencing.

You may feel trapped now and like no one cares or understands, but I can assure you they do, and I certainly do!

I get your pain.

I hear your cries and I want you to know you are not alone.

IT IS KIND OF SHOCKING WHEN
YOUR WORLD FALLS TO PIECES AND
EVERYTHING AND EVERYONE AROUND
YOU CARRIES ON WITH LIFE. HOW
CAN THE BIRDS CONTINUE TO SING?
HOW CAN PEOPLE CARRY ON LOVING
LIFE? IT IS LIKE YOU HAVE BECOME
FROZEN IN TIME AND ARE NOW
WATCHING LIFE LIKE A MOVIE. AS THE
WEEKS AND MONTHS ROLL BY, LIFE
BECOMES MORE REAL AGAIN, BUT
YOU WILL NEVER FORGET THAT POINT
IN TIME WHEN LIFE STOOD STILL.

Zoë Clark-Coates

Day 13

The darkest days of grief are the worst. For some people these days come immediately, for others they hit after the funeral, and for others they can actually come months or even years after the loss, but whenever they come, it is hard to imagine surviving them.

When you are struggling around in the darkness of grief, it is hard to know what to do to help yourself, and in the panic, it can make you feel you need to start looking at your future or changing major things about your life. I would encourage anyone who is in the darkest stages of grief to not make any big life changes. Yes, it may be tempting to quit your job, to move house, etc., etc., but now is not the time to make momentous decisions about your life. Focus on the now, survive today, and when you make it out the other side, you can then consider changes you may like to make.

TASK FOR THE DAY:

Be in the moment.

Look in a mirror and stare at your face.

Then speak to yourself, as though you are speaking to your best friend. Remind yourself how strong you are, and reassure yourself that you can and will cope with all you are enduring.

When your heart has been truly shattered, it is hard to even think of life carrying on. My best advice is to try not to think beyond the hour you are in. Grief is all-consuming, and whilst the brain is trying to process the loss, to even attempt to make plans or look at the future will simply overwhelm you. So focus on surviving the now and deal with tomorrow, tomorrow.

Zoë Clark-Coates

Day 14

You know I never believed it to be true, that people could not truly understand baby loss unless they had personally been through it. I had trained as a counsellor, and had personally walked alongside people who had lost a child so I thought I 'got it'. That was of course until I lost our first baby … then I knew I did not really have a clue. Yes, I had been able to empathise, and yes, I was able to shower down true compassion on those who had lost a child, BUT I had no idea about the depth of the pain, or how all-consuming the grief was.

There are a million words I could use to describe baby loss, but the truth of the matter is there is not one single word which would accurately explain it to someone who has not personally been through it. I think that is why it is so healing to talk with those who have been through similar experiences. It is by sharing that you can see you are not alone. There is something very reassuring when you hear someone else say 'me too'.

Task for the day:

Go onto the Saying Goodbye Facebook page or website and read stories from other people. Maybe you will feel inclined to also share your story with the team there? By seeing that other people have experienced similar things to you, I hope you will feel less alone.

ONLY SOMEONE WHO HAS LOST
A CHILD CAN TRULY RELATE TO
THE PAIN ONE GOES THROUGH
WHEN YOU LOSE A BABY YOU
HAVE CREATED AND CARRIED.

IT IS IMPOSSIBLE TO FIND
THE WORDS TO ACCURATELY
DESCRIBE IT; IT CAN ONLY BE
UNDERSTOOD BY FIRST-HAND
EXPERIENCE.

Zoë Clark-Coates

Day 15

Grief truly does come in waves. Initially it is quite hard to see that grief is like the ocean, as you can feel like you are permanently beneath the water, but as time moves on you will probably see that it is a perfect description of grief. Some days the waves are huge and come over your head, whilst other days they are gentle and you can simply step over them.

Understanding this is how grief behaves is the key to surviving it. Being aware that you will have both good and bad days removes the fear of feeling like you are suddenly back to square one when a big wave hits.

An easy mistake to make is waiting for the waves to hit, or trying to foresee the size of a wave on the horizon. The secret is to just go with the flow, and yes, I know that is so easy to say, and incredibly hard to actually do. Believe me I know … I have been there. But you will never accurately predict how the sea will behave and by trying to guess you can add to the emotional rollercoaster.

TASK FOR THE DAY:

Deal with the wave in front of you today.

If it is small be thankful and try not to worry about whether a larger one is about to arrive.

If you are facing a large wave, let it wash over you. Cry, scream or do what you need to do to survive it, but hold onto the fact it is just a wave, and you will resurface soon.

When a wave of grief hits,
it can feel overwhelming.
Hold on; you will
resurface.

Zoë Clark-Coates

Day 16

I love quotes that encourage us to mourn and to fully embrace the grieving process. I think the world often wants us to put our grief and pain in a box and pretend it is not there. If we are encouraged to grieve, it is often a prerequisite that a person should only grieve for a certain length of time, and after that time they should be fully back to normal, whatever 'normal' now is.

The truth of the matter is grieving is a personal journey. It has no set timescales and no map we can use to navigate through it. However, it is essential that we grieve fully and wholly.

Without allowing ourselves to experience raw pain, we will never fully embrace real joy and happiness. Likewise, if we spend our lives trying to avoid grief we are robbing ourselves of experiencing the good things life may have in store.

TASK FOR THE DAY:

Make a decision to not avoid grief. Make life choices based on anything but avoiding grief. Trust that you can deal with anything life throws in your lap, and do not let fear make you compromise your future plans.

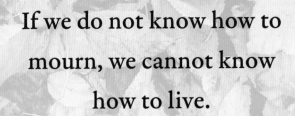

If we do not know how to
mourn, we cannot know
how to live.

Peter Marris

Day 17

Sadness is as valid as joy. I used to spend so much of my life avoiding situations that could make me unhappy, and it is only when I realised that by doing this I missed out on so much of life that I stopped. Why was I afraid of being sad? It is a horrid feeling and we would all love to feel constantly happy, but it is only when we are comfortable feeling sad, and accept it is a part of life, that we can appreciate happiness.

If I had not been to hell and back emotionally I can categorically say I would not be the joy-filled person I am today. Yes, it goes without saying of course I would prefer for the bad things to have not happened, but bad things do happen, and they happen every day to wonderful people who certainly do not deserve them. Therefore, I made the choice, and I would wholeheartedly encourage you to do the same, to not fear being sad, to just reluctantly accept that it is part of life and by facing sadness head on, we are better able to seize joy when it arrives on the horizon.

TASK FOR THE DAY:

Look at how you view sadness. What made you form the views you have on being sad? For instance, were you told as a child, 'It's not okay to cry'? Once you have determined your views, decide whether you want to remain believing that, or would like to change them. We all have the power to change our thoughts and belief systems, and I encourage everyone to use this time to become the person they long to be.

SADNESS IS AS VALID AN

EMOTION AS JOY. WITHOUT

SADNESS, WE NEVER TRULY

APPRECIATE THE MOMENTS OF

JOY LIFE THROWS IN OUR LAP.

Zoë Clark-Coates

Day 18

Often people will tell me that they are worried that they are going mad, as they find themselves wanting to keep telling their story repeatedly. I try to reassure them that this is a very normal part of the grieving process.

When a person goes through loss and trauma the brain can struggle with accepting the situation; it can become overwhelmed with feelings and of course be numb with shock. By telling your story repeatedly, it not only helps you accept what has happened, it also allows your brain time to process it.

Try to find a few individuals you can talk with, this may be your partner, a parent, a sibling or a friend, but it helps to have more than one person to talk with. Listening to the same story over and over can be quite challenging, so the more people you have to talk with, the less one person has to shoulder.

TASK FOR THE DAY:

Consider all your family and friends and decide which of them you would feel comfortable opening up to. This may seem like an easy decision, but you have to also take into account the time they have available, and also whether they will be an empathetic listener; pick wisely. I found it really helpful to reassure those I shared with that I expected nothing more from them than a listening ear, I did not need advice or even words of comfort, I just needed to feel heard.

I need to tell my story
over and over again;
it's how I begin to grasp
the enormity of my loss.

Zoë Clark-Coates

Day 19

I had no idea how much terminology and medical jargon could hurt until I lost a baby. The children we lost were referred to as products of conception, miscarriages, missed miscarriages, silent miscarriages, failed abortions, foetuses, cells, tissue … and I am sure I am missing a few here. Every time my babies were called anything other than 'a baby', I wanted to scream.

However early on in pregnancy your loss was, or however late, whether your loss was at birth, in neonatal or in early years, you lost a child, and I am so sorry for your loss.

We sadly live in a world where babies' lives are often not recognised, and where baby loss is often treated as a medical condition, rather than the loss of a life, and that in itself can add to the pain of loss.

TASK FOR THE DAY:

Try to let go of any anger you feel towards anyone who has shown disregard for your situation, or has labelled your baby anything other than a baby.

Anger and resentment can really build within us, and we often have to make a choice to forgive and move on, and this frees us to heal.

They called you
'Products of Conception'
and I said,
'No, that is my child.'

Zoë Clark-Coates

Day 20

How I wanted someone to rescue me … I would have given someone all my worldly goods to just save me from the pain. It is hard to accept that no one can be rescued from grief; it is something we have to just work through.

There are things people can do to help themselves, however. One of those things is to keep telling yourself 'you can do this', and 'you can handle it'. There is real power in words, and the more you tell yourself you cannot face it, the more you will start to truly believe it. So empower yourself, tell yourself how strong you are, and little by little, your strength will return.

TASK FOR THE DAY:

Write or print phrases you need to hear, and then stick them around your house, or in your diary.

Keep reading them, and keep speaking them out.

Truth

You know when someone made you feel that
your baby was insignificant? *They were wrong.*

You know when you were made to feel abnormal
for grieving? *They were wrong.*

You know when you were told you should just
pretend it didn't happen? *They were wrong.*

You know when you felt you were to blame?
You were wrong.

You know when you thought you were weak for not being
able to continue as normal? *You were wrong.*

You know when you felt like you had let your baby down?
You were wrong.

Your baby knew only love from the moment
they were conceived: *This is the truth.*

Your baby never knew fear, never knew sorrow,
never knew neglect: *This is the truth.*

Your baby will be your child forever. No loss, no time, and no
separation will ever change this fact.
This is the truth.

Zoë Clark-Coates

Day 21

I so needed to hear people tell me I would survive loss. I also needed to hear that people knew I was broken.

So let me tell you right now:

'You will survive this' and 'I know you are broken'.

The loss you have been through has shaken you to the very core of your soul and until now, you never knew pain like this existed. If I could personally rescue you from what you are feeling right now, I would in a heartbeat. Sadly, I cannot stop your pain, but I can tell you I understand, and I hope you feel that the words in this book bring you comfort.

I hope you can trust me when I say life will get better. Hold on, even if you only hold on by your fingertips, as soon the sun will rise and one day you will smile again.

Task for the day:

Listen to a song that brings you hope.

I personally love a song by Britt Nicole, called 'The Sun is Rising'. Let the words of whatever song you choose to listen to lift you.

I know you feel broken so I won't tell
you to have a wonderful day.
Instead, I whisper these words to you:
'Just hold on.'
As the darkest days of grief start to
lessen, the sun will rise again for you.

Zoë Clark-Coates

Day 22

I think it is very helpful to know it is okay to cry; in fact, it is okay to sob hysterically on the floor if we need to. Every tear you shed helps you move forward in the grieving process, not one is wasted.

Tears of sadness and grief are actually made of a different substance than tears of joy. How amazing is that? They have hormones and chemicals in that release the pain we are carrying. So every time we decide to have a stiff upper lip and keep those pent-up emotions locked deep within us, we are actually doing ourselves harm, tears are a natural release to help us heal.

TASK FOR THE DAY:

Allow yourself to cry.

For some crying will be an easy task, for others it could be challenging, especially if you have never given yourself permission to show emotion.

A good place to start is in the shower. As the water is falling all around you, allow your tears to become one with the water. As the water is washing over your body, your tears will be washing your soul.

Sometimes you just
need to weep on the
floor and that is okay.

Zoë Clark-Coates

Day 23

'What if' can start to haunt you. What if you had done x? What if you had not done y? What if your partner had done z? There are a million questions and a few billion potential answers, but none of them changes the situation you are now in. Sadly, when it comes to baby loss, people are often left with unanswered questions, and even the best doctors in the land can end up saying, 'It just happened, we don't know why'. Finding peace with not knowing why is a real journey, and some people never get to the place where they are okay with not knowing.

I did get to a place of feeling peaceful, and you may find it helpful to know how I got there. It is not an overnight process, and it is not something that can be forced. However, I decided I could not live constantly asking 'why?' I could choose to accept that so many things happen in the world that are hard to understand. My five babies died, I have no idea why, but I am also very grateful they lived. Yes, they never knew life outside the womb, but they still lived.

TASK FOR THE DAY:

It may be hard to believe that by simply making a choice to accept that bad things do happen, can extinguish the big 'what if', but it really can, and when you get to that place of peace, it is a real gift. Today, try to make that decision if you feel ready. You may have to make it again and again, but try to accept so many things happen in this life, and often we will not ever know why.

WHEN YOU LOSE A CHILD,

YOU CAN BE TRAPPED IN

A WORLD OF 'WHAT IF?'

Zoë Clark-Coates

Day 24

I really feared loss would define me. I worried that I would be that woman who had lost five babies. I then realised we all have a choice as to what defines us, we have the power to tell the world what we are, and we do not have to let the world tell us.

So how do we refuse to be defined by the experiences we have been through? Well I guess the most important way is to fully grieve, and allow ourselves to heal. If we are stuck in grief, it is easy for our losses to define us, because that is all people will see when they interact with us. However, if we move through grief, those around us will see us as whole people, and they will not be able to limit us to a specific period of our lives.

TASK FOR THE DAY:

Consider how you want the world to see you.

What personality traits would you like to be recognised in you, and how would you like to be spoken about in your absence?

Then consider how you can help make that happen.

When you survive loss
everyone is quick to tell you how
strong you are, and how tough you
must be. But actually, no one has a
choice to survive grief do they? It's not
optional. You just have to cry in the
shower, sob into your pillow and pray
you will make it.

Zoë Clark-Coates

Day 25

Some people lack compassion or empathy, and no amount of talking, explaining or showing them the error of their ways will change them, so you have to decide if you want to remain friends with them. If the answer is yes, accept that this is how they are and ensure you set your boundaries high, so they cannot constantly hurt you. If the answer is no, end the friendship and find other people to share your life with.

The crucial thing when you have non-empathetic relationships is to be careful what you share. If you constantly pour out your heart to them, with the hope that they may give you the response you are looking for, you are opening yourself up for more hurt.

I personally have many friends I would not have a heart to heart with. This may be because I am aware they lack the levels of compassion I need when talking about personal things, but it may also be because I know they are the type of person to feel they need to fix anything they hear, rather than just being willing to sit and listen.

Task for the day:

Look at your life and consider whether the people you are sharing with are helping you, or causing you more pain. If you find some people are hurting you because of their responses, make a decision to limit what you share with them.

SOME PEOPLE HAVE A NATURAL
ABILITY TO MAKE OTHERS FEEL
RUBBISH ABOUT THEMSELVES.

YOU HAVE TO DECIDE WHETHER
YOU ALLOW THIS OR NOT, AS NO
ONE CAN MAKE YOU FEEL BAD
WITHOUT YOUR PERMISSION.

SO SET YOUR BOUNDARY
LINES HIGH AND WATCH YOUR
HAPPINESS LEVELS RISE.

Zoë Clark-Coates

Day 26

Boy does it hurt when those around us do not acknowledge our pain. It can almost feel like they are telling us our grief and suffering does not matter or is unimportant. The trouble is we cannot control how others respond or behave, all we can do is be careful how we react, and treat others like we want to be treated.

So how should you respond, if—for instance—your sister-in-law is acting as if you have never lost a baby? There is no black and white answer to this, and there is no right or wrong way to respond. Some may feel it is right to confront the sister-in-law and explain how her behaviour is making them feel. Someone else may feel it is best to ignore the behaviour, or perhaps even avoid seeing the sister-in-law. What I will say is, do what is best for you, but also try to remember that unless you have been through loss, you have no idea what it is like, so often people behave from ignorance, rather than from being mean.

Task for the day:

Does anyone in your life repeatedly hurt you with how they respond to your grief? Consider how you can stop this from happening. Could you write a letter explaining your feelings, could you have a heart to heart with them? Take time to plan what you will say, and pick the moment wisely. Remember, do not attack them for how they are; just explain what you need from them.

By not acknowledging
someone's grief, you are
telling them their suffering
doesn't matter.

Zoë Clark-Coates

Day 27

When you lose a baby, so many people tell you how brave you are. So often, in fact, you may start to want to scream, 'I'm not brave, I have no choice, I am just surviving'. Everyone told me I was brave. I was brave to go back to work. I was brave to keep trying for more children. I was brave for being able to smile. Looking back maybe all of that is brave, maybe it is easier to just give in and give up, but I certainly did not feel brave, and I am guessing you do not either.

I think what most people are trying to say when they utter these words, is 'I couldn't do what you are doing'. You see, losing a baby has to be up there with one of the worst things a human can go through, and I too felt 'I could never cope with losing a baby' before I was forced to do just that.

TASK FOR THE DAY:

When you hear those words that you are brave, try to accept them and not reject them. Realise you are brave. You are amazing. You are making the choice to not only survive this, but to thrive and that is a heroic thing to do.

People kept saying I was brave. I fought the desire to laugh each time it was said. I felt far from brave. I was scared. I was terrified. I was holding my breath to see if I could even survive the journey I was forced to walk.

Zoë Clark-Coates

Day 28

It can be hard to be truthful, really truthful. It is easier to make an excuse for how we look, or for the lack of joy we are expressing. Why is this? I think at times it is for our own benefit, it is kind of exhausting having to constantly explain what we are feeling and why we feel it, so often it is easier to just respond to the 'How are you?' question with a 'I'm fine, thank you.' I think we also often want to protect the other party from the truth of our response. When we ask someone, 'How are you feeling today?' we expect a standard reply, don't we? A simple, 'Great, thanks'. Are we ever ready for a really true reply, like 'Things are utterly terrible actually. Last night I honestly didn't think I could carry on living any more'?

So what should we do? Well, first and foremost, whenever we ask someone how they are, let us be open to any response and encourage people to be real with their reply. Secondly, let us make a choice to always answer honestly. This does not mean giving everyone a thesis on where we are currently at in life, it just means instead of saying something we feel is expected, stop, and think and give an honest reply.

TASK FOR THE DAY:

When you are asked how you are today, tell them how you really are. If that means you say things are really tough, say that. If things are better than they were yesterday, say that. But be real.

The day after we lost our baby, a friend
visited us. She sat on my bed and held my
hand and said, 'It happened to me too.'
At that moment I realised, connecting
with another person who has walked a
similar path changes the journey of grief.
We don't need to walk alone.

Zoë Clark-Coates

Day 29

Grief can truly show people what is important in life. Superficial things quickly feel just 'superficial'. At the early stages of grief, I did not want there to be any benefits from what we were going through. How could anything good come out of such tragedy and pain? Surely if something good came out of it, then it would mean that it is a good thing my baby died. However, as I came through that darkness, I realised the exact opposite to be true. When good things come out of a harrowing circumstance that is a blessing. It never justifies that loss, but it is a gift that can live on from it.

The best way to explain this is to imagine an organ donor. A woman decides to donate the organs of her husband following a car accident. One organ goes to a father of two who would not have lived for more than a month without receiving it. The fact that this man's heart has saved someone, is a gift and a blessing. However, it in no way makes it okay that the man whose heart was donated died, for he too had a life, and had children he needed to take care of. The same applies when good things come out of our grief, none of those things make it okay that our babies died, these are just the gifts our children have brought us.

TASK FOR THE DAY:

What gifts has grief brought you? Take some time to consider how grateful you are for these blessings. It may be that you are waiting for good things to come from your loss, and that is okay, just be willing to accept that good things can come from tragic events.

I HAVE NEVER KNOWN ANYTHING

AS EFFECTIVE AS GRIEF AT

SHOWING YOU WHAT TRULY

MATTERS IN LIFE. IT HAS A WAY

OF REVEALING THE TRUTH AND

REINFORCING THE VALUE OF THE

PEOPLE AROUND YOU.

Zoë Clark-Coates

Day 30

Loss really showed me how blessed I was to have true friends in my life, but I am fully aware not everyone is so fortunate. You may be like me and have been surrounded by caring and compassionate friends, or you may have sadly found that none of your friends were real friends; they were actually just people you happened to be doing life with.

If you are blessed to have great friends, I urge you to keep nurturing these friendships and never take them for granted.

If you have now found yourself in a place where you need to make new friends, my advice would be to look for people who have walked a similar path to you. Some of my dearest friends have also lost babies and that has built a depth of friendship I could never have dreamed of. It is much better to have something deeply meaningful in common, than a shared love of the same music.

Task for the day:

If you have good friends, send them a message to thank them for being supportive. If you need to find new friends, consider how you can meet new people, and take the first steps.

When a friend walks
beside us as we
journey through grief,
it is the greatest gift
anyone could ask for.

Zoë Clark-Coates

Day 31

When you are grieving, it can be hard to watch what you are saying and the manner in which you are saying it. So many things appear futile and almost irrelevant, so it is easy to appear irritated or short-tempered. It is good to be aware of this, so you can try to be careful, and it is wise to alert family and friends that if you slip up it is nothing personal.

I personally found taking time out, and having personal space helped me cope with general conversation, and it stopped me feeling overwhelmed by day-to-day chatter.

TASK FOR THE DAY:

Try to take some personal time and do something you enjoy.

Maybe it is sitting and reading for thirty minutes. Maybe it is baking.

When people feel sad or low they often give up on the things that bring them pleasure, so I really encourage you to keep doing the things that brought you happiness in the past.

Hold no man
responsible for
what he says in
his grief.

The Talmud

Day 32

I really struggled with the reality that my babies had gone, and what compounded those feelings was that in some people's minds my children never even existed, as they had not been born. This is a common issue for many people who have lost a baby through miscarriage. A common issue for those who have lost a child at birth is that those who have not had a chance to meet or hold their child can often think of their baby as just a loss, and not as a son or daughter.

The bottom line is we cannot instantly change the world, and sadly, we cannot alter everyone's attitudes towards babies that are lost, so all we can do is try to be patient, and educate all those we speak to.

TASK FOR THE DAY:

Try to write down on paper what your lost baby means to you. If one day you feel comfortable to share it with others, do.

When people hear heartfelt eulogies, they get a real insight into the pain of loss.

Say not in grief
'He is no more'
but live in
thankfulness
that 'He was'.

Hebrew Proverb

Day 33

We all need to hear 'well done' from time to time. We also need to hear that we have the ability to survive whatever we are facing. So today let me say to you 'well done' and 'keep going'.

I often wanted to curl into a ball and hide away, the only thing that stopped me was that even when I was curled in a ball, it hurt just as badly. However, it takes real strength to keep going. I want to reassure you it is super common to want to hide away, and sometimes even normal every day activities can feel challenging. Getting dressed and brushing your hair for some people seems impossible, and it is okay to not bother for a few days, but there comes a time when we need to step back into daily life, and at least take care of ourselves. The best place to start is by showering and getting dressed each day, and trying to eat regularly. Gradually add in additional things. I adore make-up and the process of getting ready for the day, but post loss I felt almost guilty for doing it. Therefore, for weeks I did not go near a lipstick or mascara. To me, looking presentable and made-up said to the world, 'I am fine now, and I have forgotten about my baby'. Of course, it did no such thing, but grief can make us irrational, and we have to try to overcome any illogical behaviours as we move through the grieving process.

TASK FOR THE DAY:

Get dressed in your favourite outfit. It is tempting to give up on yourself and your appearance post loss, but today wear something that makes you feel confident and good.

I don't want friends who just
like to sit with me in the good
times. I look for people who will
come searching for me if I am
quiet, those who if they find me
down a hole, will get a ladder
and climb in to sit with me.
Real friends do life with you.
The good, the bad and the ugly.

Zoë Clark-Coates

Day 34

It is difficult to stay in the present, especially post loss. When your heart's desire is to have a baby it is hard to not think about your future and when, and if, you will be blessed with a child to raise. Those around us often fail to give us the space to take time off from thinking about having future children. Post our losses, people often said to me, 'At least you know you can have children, will you try again straight away?' I know this question comes from a place of wanting to be supportive, but when you have just lost a baby, it is hard to hear. What I actually heard from that comment was, 'You should not be grieving, because you should be thankful you are not infertile. If you stop grieving, you can just replace the baby you lost.' It would probably horrify anyone who said this to me, to know that this is what I heard, as it would definitely not have been what they were meaning, but words can be hurtful and people do need to select them wisely.

We also should not be rushed into thinking about future babies. You do not need to decide right now whether you want to try for more children. In fact, any decision you make will probably change twenty times over as you move through the grieving process, so just take time to heal.

TASK FOR THE DAY:

Think of how to best answer someone if they ask you, 'Are you going to have more children?' Having a prepared answer takes off the pressure in the moment. I used to say, 'We have no idea, only time will tell,' and change the subject.

People are often quick to envy others for the life they have, but what if they only have a happy life due to the rocky path they have walked? What if they only have children following years of tragic loss? What if they only experience so much joy because they grabbed hold of happiness with both hands, following years of harrowing pain? Would you still envy the life they now lead? Perhaps the grass is only greener as it has been watered with tears.

Day 35

The most common question I hear is probably 'Is there a fast-track option to speed up grief?' Wow, I wish I could answer 'Yes'! Imagine if we could grieve and recover in a day or even a month. Sadly, this is not the case; grief is a slow and steady process. However, there are ways we can move through it more freely.

The way to not be stuck in grief is to face it head on. Do not run from the pain, or hide from the struggle, just bravely confront the agony and allow all the complex feelings to be processed. By doing this you will steadily move forwards and come through the rawest part of grief.

TASK FOR THE DAY:

Try to write about the pain you have felt. Journaling your experiences can really help you process the trauma of loss, and it can also help you see how far you have come, when you read back over previous things you have written.

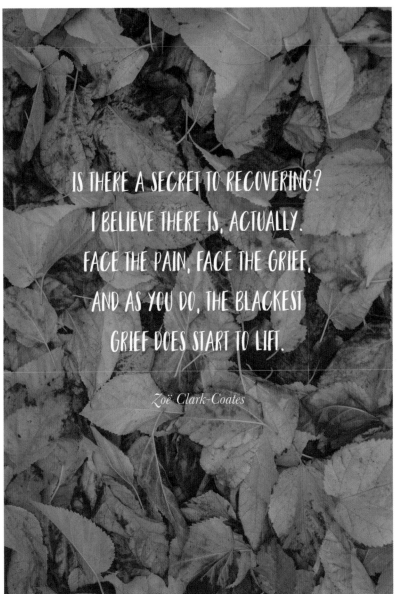

IS THERE A SECRET TO RECOVERING?
I BELIEVE THERE IS, ACTUALLY.
FACE THE PAIN, FACE THE GRIEF,
AND AS YOU DO, THE BLACKEST
GRIEF DOES START TO LIFT.

Zoë Clark-Coates

Day 36

Grief is a lifelong journey. When I initially heard that, it scared me to death. I thought it meant I would feel this depth of pain and would be in a state of mourning until the day I die. However, it does not mean that at all. Let me try to explain.

In the days and months that follow loss, we are in a mourning period. I also refer to this time as the darkest days of grief. Some people do remain in a state of mourning forever, and those people are usually stuck in a stage of grief. However, most people move through the mourning period, and the pain becomes far less raw, and they can even smile rather than cry when they think of the baby they lost.

So why is grieving a lifelong journey? The reason is that we never get over the loss of a loved one, or forget them. They carry on being part of us and part of our lives forever, so we will always grieve for them not being with us, but the pain doesn't remain exactly the same, it is ever changing, and often hurts more at certain times than at other times.

TASK FOR THE DAY:

Consider how grief has changed you; also, look at how you would like it to change you more. For me grief changed me into a more appreciative person, it also stopped me taking things for granted.

I used to think grief was a set period of time,

following the loss of someone you cared for.

I now know it's no such thing.

Grief is a lifelong journey

and it is also a master sculptor.

It chisels us, sometimes with harsh blows,

and at other times, delicate taps.

Over time we become new people.

We feel differently and we act differently.

Once we accept that we can

never go back to being how we were,

life stops being so scary.

We stop fighting to hold onto the old,

and we can truly embrace the new.

Zoë Clark-Coates

Day 37

Facing special occasions or global celebrations such as Christmas can be such a challenge for people who are grieving. Everyone around us being so happy can exacerbate the pain we are feeling.

So how do we face them?

Well, everyone has multiple options, and you should always do what is best for you.

Option one would be to avoid them. For some this can be the easiest way to handle the situation, for others it can actually be the hardest, as it can mean family or friends apply pressure or guilt on you for missing occasions.

The second option can be to attend the events, but tell everyone who is attending that it will be a challenge for you, and they should not be offended or upset if you are less enthusiastic or more withdrawn than usual.

For me the second option was the one I always selected, and it actually worked well for me. Because I told people to not expect 'happy Zoë', I felt free to just be me and I did not need to apply a fake smile. I will add that I did say to people, if they felt by me being 'real' I may ruin the event, I was one hundred percent fine with not attending and would not take it personally, this gave people the option to say, maybe on this occasion it would be better for you to not attend.

TASK FOR THE DAY:

Boundaries are a hard thing to set, especially when it comes to relationships and stating what is or is not acceptable. Some may struggle in day-to-day life with this, so it is even harder when we are grieving. Try to be clear on what people can expect from you, as by doing that you have the freedom to be you.

THERE WILL ALWAYS BE

STOCKINGS MISSING FROM OUR

FIREPLACE EVERY CHRISTMAS.

TIME AND LIFE MOVING ON WILL

NEVER CHANGE THIS FACT.

Zoë Clark-Coates

Day 38

It is very easy to get into a pattern of criticising ourselves, and constantly berating ourselves about how we acted or responded pre, during or post loss, but we should all stop doing it. Now I am not saying we should not be aware of our behaviour, as we definitely should. And I am not saying we should not be trying to constantly improve and better ourselves as people, as again I think that is crucially important, but being full of self-condemnation does neither of these things, it just makes us feel insignificant and like a failure.

We need to be empowering ourselves to be better, and we also need to take pride in how we handle situations, and how we manage to stand up again, after falling.

TASK FOR THE DAY:

Make a list of all the things you do well, and all the things you are proud of. This may seem like a simple task, but it is surprisingly difficult to give ourselves a pat on the back.

Next look at how you have handled loss. What are you proud of regarding your journey?

Today when you criticise yourself
for not being happy enough,
for not being chatty enough,
stop and remember the
heartache you have endured.
Instead of condemnation, feel pride.
Pride that you are still standing.
Pride that the grief that could
have destroyed you, has actually
made you more compassionate,
more caring, and a kinder human.

Zoë Clark-Coates

Day 39

It is hard to find the words to explain grief, loss and bereavement, isn't it? It is easy to worry that any words one uses almost minimise the experience, and so it can feel much simpler to remain silent.

How can anyone quickly and concisely say that 'losing a baby shatters you and makes the world seem irrelevant?'

What I want to encourage you to do, however, is to keep talking, no matter how hard it is to find the words. Any words are better than no words, and by talking about baby loss we break the taboo. We also send the message to everyone that it is okay to talk, and it is good to talk, which means your friends and family are likely to open up if they have been through such an experience.

TASK FOR THE DAY:

Try to think of how you could describe loss to someone.

By having pre-prepared answers, it means you will be less taken off guard when you are asked.

When we lost our baby, we didn't
know the language to use to explain
the pain, the loss, the utter agony
we were experiencing. Over time,
we found some words that aptly
verbalised the grief, but what we
learnt was that there are simply
no words to describe baby loss;
it goes beyond the vocabulary
available to us all.

Zoë Clark-Coates

Day 40

Grief and bereavement are common occurrences in life, and as such, most people have an opinion of how to best deal with it. Whilst this can be helpful and useful (if good advice is offered), it can also be very unhelpful if a person is forceful with their advice, or takes it upon themselves to critique the way you are dealing with your loss.

If you find yourself on the receiving end of unhelpful advice, I have found a great way of dealing with it is reverse psychology. I say something like, 'Of course, you will be aware that every loss is unique, and what works for one person may not work for another'. I then compliment them on how they have managed to survive loss and lived to tell the tale, and try to change the subject fast. There are some discussions that just are not helpful to have whilst in mourning, and debates on how best to handle grief are definitely up there with things to avoid.

Task for the day:

Look at what things have helped, or are helping you the most at this time, and consider why that is. Can you do more of them?

Some people have a lot of expectations of how others should grieve. Remember you do not need to live up to any of these. This is your journey. Walk it your way.

Zoë Clark-Coates

Day 41

Grief can feel utterly overwhelming, especially if you consider what a big mountain it actually is.

In the early days of grief, I would often be consumed with panic at the thought of the road I needed to walk. It seemed almost impossible that I could walk through the grief and be at a place of peace again, and the more I looked at what I needed to process to get to that place, the more the panic grew.

The best advice I can offer is, do not focus on the summit, just look at the next step. Also, do not compare your walk with anyone else's. So often people say, 'Why can't I be at the same place as that person?', when that other person set off up the mountain months earlier. In addition, everyone's story of loss is different, which means everyone's mountains are different sizes. So focus on your journey and take it a step at a time.

How would you describe the mountain you are walking?

Grief can feel like a
mountain in front of you.
Try not to focus on the
summit, just concentrate
on the steps immediately
ahead of you.

Zoë Clark-Coates

Day 42

It really is the greatest gift to know we have been heard, and to know our heartache has been recognised.

I will never forget the times friends and family took time out from their lives to sit with me and share their stories of loss, or listened to me retelling my story repeatedly. Though those times were exceptionally painful and raw, they were also truly beautiful. When we connect at heart level with people something magical happens; our souls resonate with one another, and to know we are understood—really understood—is a very special feeling.

If you are cautious of opening up your life to people at this level, can I at least encourage you to try with one person? Find one person you can trust, and set some time aside to have a heart to heart, as it may be so helpful to you, and could be a gift to the other person.

TASK FOR THE DAY:

Talk with someone you trust, and share with them something you have not told anyone else.

TO KNOW SOMEONE HAS HEARD YOUR
CRIES AND SEEN YOUR PAIN IS MORE
THAN A GIFT, IT'S LIFE CHANGING.

Zoë Clark-Coates

Day 43

'Am I still a mother if my baby died?'—Yes!

Likewise, 'Am I still a father if my baby died?'—Yes!

When you create a child you become a parent whether you like it or not. A baby does not suddenly become a person when it is born; it is a person when it starts growing within a woman. This means you are a parent as soon as you have conceived a child.

One of the hardest parts of baby loss is not being recognised as a parent just because you are carrying your child in your heart instead of your arms, but I want to reassure you: 'You are a parent'.

So how do we get the world to recognise all parents as parents, even if they do not have a child with them to raise? Well that is a challenge. I think all people can do is keep sharing personal stories, and keep telling those around them that they are a parent with empty arms.

TASK FOR THE DAY:

Try to write a poem or even a statement about the challenges of being left with empty arms.

I don't even know if I understood
the concept of hell on earth, until
I journeyed through grief and loss.
When all feels helpless, when the
world feels dark and you pray that
you won't wake up each day, that's
hell on earth. When you survive it,
life is forever changed.

Zoë Clark-Coates

Day 44

It is imperative that we deal with grief and process it. There is a famous saying that, 'If we don't let grief out, it makes our internal organs weep', and it is so true. If we try to repress grief, it can have serious knock-on effects on our health. Depression, gut problems and fertility issues are all commonly reported by people who have not dealt with grief.

There are so many ways to face grief and to help your brain process it, and I encourage everyone to do so.

Here are a few things which can help:

Keep a diary/journal—write about your feelings, the pain, and the loss.

Art therapy—do you like drawing or painting? Producing art which explains your pain, or visually represents your suffering, can be a great outlet.

Poetry—do you like poems or writing? Writing poems is a brilliant outlet for grief, as you can say things in poems that are hard to say in other mediums.

TASK FOR THE DAY:

Try a different outlet for expressing your grief, something you may have not used before. Maybe you have not produced any artwork since school, well now is a great time to have a go.

Grief can make people feel
very uncomfortable ... but
do you know what's worse?

Being the one grieving.

Zoë Clark-Coates

Day 45

Grief can remove your confidence! I have seen the most outgoing people lose all confidence overnight following the loss of a baby. Why can this happen? Well, loss shakes us to the core and having something traumatic happen can make us question who we are, what we do, and where we are heading.

I know for me having everything in my world be 'okay' one moment, and then the bottom falling from beneath me minutes later, made me feel very insecure. It made me fearful of life. How could I now feel secure in the world, when I was acutely aware that something so earth shattering could happen at any moment?

It is also common to feel unworthy, and not special. This can come about just from the heaviness of grief, but it can also happen because of how a person was treated through their loss.

So how do we rebuild confidence? It takes time, and the amount of time is different for every person. The secret is to take it slowly, and to face any fears that are now a stumbling block for you, and eventually you will regain any lost confidence, and possibly gain some extra on top.

TASK FOR THE DAY:

Consider whether loss has made you less confident. If it has, list the things you now feel scared of, and decide which of those you would most like to overcome first. Next consider little changes you could make which would force you to face those fears.

Sometimes people
lie and tell you they
are fine. Dig a little
deeper and you will
find their pillow is
soaked with tears.

Zoë Clark-Coates

Day 46

It is amazing how many people treat miscarriage and baby loss as just a medical incident. One day someone is pregnant, and the next they are not. So the pregnancy just stopped, right? Wrong. The person lost a child, or perhaps multiple children.

Whilst most losses happen in the home and do not really involve doctors and hospitals, sometimes it is necessary for people to be treated by medical personnel or to have a hospital stay. How they are treated whilst being cared for becomes a momentous part of their journey through loss.

I would love for us to live in a world where everyone gets first class care, and is treated like what they are, a bereaved parent, but I am acutely aware that most countries have a long way to go in improving their post-loss care programmes.

If you had wonderful, compassionate care, I am so pleased for you. However, if you are amongst the majority of people who have had a poor standard of care, I am so sorry.

My hope is that in the not-too-distant future, everyone will be treated with love and compassion, but until then we just have to deal with the extra trauma that bad care causes.

Please know, however you were treated and whatever experience you have had, I recognise your bereavement as the loss of a child, and so do millions of others around the world.

TASK FOR THE DAY:

How do you feel you were treated through your loss? Was it good or bad? If you experienced great care or bad care, would you consider writing to tell the people that provided it about your experience? This can really help change the care system.

YOU KNOW WHEN IT HURTS
LIKE HELL TO TALK AND SAY
HOW YOU FEEL? WELL, THAT'S
EXACTLY WHEN YOU SHOULD
SHARE YOUR FEELINGS. PAIN
CAN START TO HEAL WHEN
IT'S EXPRESSED.

Zoë Clark-Coates

Day 47

Giving up. Tempting, isn't it? When things just seem too hard, and it feels almost impossible to imagine living another day. I have been there; I have felt that. I used to cry out to God to end my suffering, and beg Him to let me go home to heaven where I would be with my babies.

If you too are currently in that place, I am aware that very few words may be able to reach you, until some of the rawest pain you are feeling dissipates, but I hope you can hear these words.

It is going to get better, the ferocious, all-consuming grief you are experiencing will lessen, and that will happen sooner than you can imagine.

I do not know the exact day I woke up and the weight of grief was just a little lighter, but I know it happened. Then a while later the weight reduced again, and that's how it continued, gradually getting smaller and smaller, until my will to live outweighed my will to be in heaven.

So be patient, hold on, I know it feels like you are treading water, but it is worth it and one day you will see that.

TASK FOR THE DAY:

Be still, listen to some relaxing music and simply imagine the weight of grief being lifted from you.

I didn't know if it was true that one could die from a broken heart. In the depth of my grief, I hoped it was true. The thought of not having to live another day, carrying the darkest of grief, was at times the only glimmer of light on the horizon. But I did not die, I lived. Whilst the journey I took was agony, the path did lead me to the most glorious place of joy. Today I celebrate the children I carried and live a life they would be proud of.

Zoë Clark-Coates

Day 48

It is pretty earth-shaking when we have to accept the love for our baby won't keep them alive. Wouldn't it be amazing if it could, though, if the love we have for any person could sustain them?

I could not believe I could be given the gift of carrying a child, only to lose them before I even held them in my arms. How cruel life can be, but at the same time how beautiful.

When we finally accept that no life is guaranteed to continue, it can really rock the core of our being, and it can make us view life very differently. For me, this discovery made me seize life with two hands. I was determined to make a difference with the small amount of time I had on this earth.

TASK FOR THE DAY:

Consider how your loss will drive you forward to make a difference in the world. Could you donate time to a charity, perhaps The Mariposa Trust? Could you help at a local soup kitchen? What I can tell you is this, by giving back to society, it will help you, and you will be rewarded by far greater measures than the time you donate.

I truly believed the love for
my child would save their
life. I was not prepared to
say goodbye.

Zoë Clark-Coates

Day 49

My favourite people are those who have at some time been broken. Something special happens to people who have walked through the fire, and come out of it with a heart to help others, or a passion to make a difference in the world. People who have suffered are more compassionate, more caring, and often have their priorities in the right order. They also make the greatest friends.

Loss changed me radically. It changed me for the better, and I hope you will one day feel the same about yourself.

How can you make grief change you for the better? You need to choose to. A simple choice, to allow all the suffering you have been through to make you more caring and kind, is the catalyst that starts the process. You need to follow it with actions, but that can happen further down the line when you feel much stronger.

TASK FOR THE DAY:

How would you like grief to change you for the better? Consider how you can start making that a reality even if it is in the future.

If you ask me who I like to spend time with, I would tell you this: let me sit amongst those who have known suffering, those who have been to hell and back as they waded through the valley of despair. They are the ones who wear their heart on their sleeve. They hate polite chit-chat, as they know life is far too short for superficial conversation. They speak about issues that truly matter, and they connect with others deeply. They value people, and when they make a friend, it is a friend for life. Why? Well, pain reveals people and it shines a light on things that matter. My advice to anyone is search out these people and make them your best friends. They will make your life better simply be being in it.

Zoë Clark-Coates

Day 50

Baby loss is synonymous with waiting. Waiting for scans, waiting for news, waiting for results, waiting for labour, waiting for delivery, waiting for the shock to diminish, waiting, waiting, waiting.

Maybe you are now past the waiting stage, but if you are in the middle of a wait, what advice can I offer? For every person different things will help, but a great thing for most people is distraction, and I know this sounds almost ridiculously simple, but if you can focus on something else for an hour, for a few hours, it helps time feel like it's passing more quickly.

If you are able to work, then work. If you are able to get absorbed into a TV series, do that. Whatever it is, let your mind be consumed by something other than 'waiting'. I got out an old box set of a favourite TV show and started to re-watch it from the very first episode, not the most productive way to spend a hundred hours, but it got me through. Find something, anything that helps you survive the wait.

TASK FOR THE DAY:

Find something that you can get absorbed into when you need to wait, or just so you can relax and take time out from thinking.

Waiting to hear if my baby had died was like sitting on the edge of a volatile volcano. I was hopeful that it would not erupt, but acutely aware that if it did, my life would feel like it was over. Hours felt like days, and days like weeks. Then the moment came, the doctor told me the findings from my scan. My baby had died. Within seconds the volcano erupted; hot lava covered everything. The person I had been was gone forever, and it took a long time for the new me to emerge from the ashes.

Zoë Clark-Coates

Day 51

Death does not end the relationship with anyone, and certainly not with the baby or children you have lost. You will forever be their parent, and they will always be carried in your heart.

I think when you can accept this, it helps a little with the pain of loss. To think of the relationship as over, as finished, makes it final, and that brings an added layer of pain, but it is not like that at all.

When you lose a baby your relationship with your child just changes, from that in the present that can be seen, to a relationship in the heart, which can only be felt.

TASK FOR THE DAY:

If you feel able, write a letter to your baby, telling them about the gifts they have brought to you.

Today someone went for a scan.
They were full of expectation,
Beside themselves with excitement,
Overflowing with hope.
Today that person was told their baby had died.
They had minutes to gather the pieces of their heart off the scan
room floor before they were asked to leave, as another expectant
mum was needing to have their scan.
They walked out of the hospital feeling broken,
Auto-drive clicked in,
Somehow they found their way home.
At their front door, they found the key and let themselves in.
The house felt so different to a few hours before,
Like a magic wand was waved and all joy vanished from the world.
Empty, Confused, Frightened,
A million unanswered questions running through their mind.
Waves of tears, Silent screams, Then numb.
Waves of fresh tears, More silent screams.
In ten minutes, they went from the top of the mountain,
to the valley of distress.
This is loss. This is reality.
This is why The Mariposa Trust exists.

Zoë Clark-Coates

Day 52

Fear can be the elephant in the room after your loss, and it does not even need to be fear connected to babies or fertility etc. It can be fear of leaving the house, fear of returning to work, fear of meeting up with friends.

Home can quickly become your safety net when fear steps in and even the thought of stepping out the door can be just too much to handle. If this is the case for you, the best way to deal with it is by finding support. That support could come from a charity like The Mariposa Trust (sayinggoodbye.org), or it could come from your doctor, or a friend or family member, but you do need support. The horrid thing about this type of fear is it tends to build and increase if it is not faced, and the longer you leave it, the worse it feels to overcome it. It is good if you can face it head on as quickly as possible.

TASK FOR THE DAY:

Have you developed any fears since you went through loss? If yes, how can you overcome them? Do you need help, or do you feel able to face them alone?

BABY LOSS CAN
MAKE PEOPLE FEAR
EVERYTHING. SUDDENLY
THE WORST THING IN THE
WORLD HAS HAPPENED,
AND THIS CAN MAKE
THEM FEAR BOTH BIG
AND SMALL THINGS.
THIS IS WHEN THEY NEED
FRIENDS AND FAMILY TO
REASSURE THEM AND
BRING THEM COMFORT.

Zoë Clark-Coates

Day 53

Feeling as if you want to be protected is totally normal and common after your loss; often people say they feel like a child again. The world seems bigger and scarier, and they hope that people will not talk to them if they enter the room.

I also often hear people say they just want to become invisible.

All of these feelings are normal and they will pass. They happen because a person feels out of control. They are suddenly aware that there is nothing they can do to stop the feelings or the circumstance they are facing, and the last time they felt like this was as a child, when they were subject to their parents' choices.

If you feel like this, it will pass, but it is good to inform those who love and support you that you are feeling this, as it gives them the opportunity to carry you emotionally for a while.

Explain to them where you struggle most, if it is when people ask you what has happened, maybe ask your partner to do the explaining initially.

For some people it can be helpful to develop a secret code word. You can say it if you are struggling and need rescuing and your partner will know to help you get out of the situation without any further explanation.

TASK FOR THE DAY:

Do you feel you want to be protected? Are those around you aware of this? If not make them aware today.

After losing a baby,

people can feel

lost, scared, and an

overwhelming need

to be protected.

Zoë Clark-Coates

Day 54

Guilt for feeling okay or just numb is normal.

I speak with so many people who worry that this means they are unfeeling, or uncaring, or may make other people think this about them. Some people worry that sitting and crying shows a lack of restraint. Others, who are not sitting in the corner sobbing, worry this means they are not truly connecting with their full emotions. Again, this comes back to the fact that everyone deals with grief differently, and everything is okay. You set the rules, no one else.

For some people, sticking with their daily routine is the only way they feel able to survive, and they continue as if they are on auto drive. As the shock lifts and the reality of what has happened sinks in, they will often start to open up, sometimes at the oddest of times. This can take them and others by surprise, but it is important that they keep talking once they feel able.

TASK FOR THE DAY:

Explain in a letter or journal how you feel you have processed your grief. If you could choose to process it differently, would you? If yes, how so?

IT IS TOTALLY NORMAL TO HAVE
YOUR EMOTIONS GOING HAYWIRE,
AND IT'S JUST AS NORMAL TO
HAVE YOUR EMOTIONS BE
TOTALLY ABSENT.

Zoë Clark-Coates

Day 55

The grief cloud can come thick and fast, or slow and steady, and often people fear it is depression descending on them. Grief, however, is very different to depression, though it has obvious similarities. A person who is depressed, like a person who is in mourning, can feel hopeless, they can also feel exhausted and tearful.

So how do you know whether you need extra help from your doctor? The answer is if you are even thinking you may be depressed, you need to speak to your GP. GPs are experts in assessing what is or is not depression, and when you are in grief it is very hard to make that judgment call yourself.

The most important thing is to know there is support out there, and if a doctor does not show the level of support you expect or hope for, you should see a different doctor.

TASK FOR THE DAY:

How would you describe grief? Has it felt like a cloud to you? It may be helpful to write down your experiences.

In the darkest days of grief,
you may feel like you have been
absorbed into a black cloud.
This is normal, and by allowing
yourself to grieve, the cloud
will slowly lift.

Zoë Clark-Coates

Day 56

Who am I now?

This is a question so many people ask themselves as they emerge from grief and loss.

I know I am a very different person after losing five babies. Some people find the changes in themselves a positive thing; others feel they are now fumbling around in the darkness to rediscover who they are.

Whilst it can be scary to have your life stripped back and your motivations, goals and future plans laying in a heap of confusion, loss does present you with an opportunity to pick up all those things you remain passionate about. It gives you a chance to dismiss and disregard those things that no longer seem relevant or important.

Task for the day:

Write a list of all the things that used to be important to you and the goals you had.

Now write a second list of the things that are important to you now, and your new goals and dreams.

Spend time considering how you can achieve these new goals in honour of your lost baby/ies.

Grief can make you lose your identity. As you grieve, the new you will emerge, but be patient—this does not happen overnight.

Zoë Clark-Coates

Day 57

When you find out you are pregnant it is hard to think of anything else, isn't it?

Your mind becomes instantly taken over. You can be standing in line at the supermarket, and all you are thinking is, 'Wow, I am pregnant.'

Maybe it is because our brains and bodies know we are the only protector of the baby that this happens, and it is to ensure we make the right choices about what we eat, and what activities we partake in. However, it becomes a massive issue if we lose the child we are carrying. Our mind still remains all-consumed by the baby we were once carrying. It is like once this switch is pulled, it is hard to reverse it, and it makes grieving the loss so much more painful, as there is no escape from the constant thoughts.

It takes a few months for this to change, but eventually it does. One day you start thinking about other things, and the void that appeared in your brain is slowly filled.

TASK FOR THE DAY:

Today allow yourself time to relax and have the freedom to think of anything you want. Maybe you want to take time to think about your baby, or maybe you want to think of something totally different, like an amazing holiday you once had? Whatever you think about, take the space you need.

From the moment I discovered

I was pregnant, I was constantly

thinking of the baby I was

carrying. From the moment

I discovered my baby had died,

I was constantly thinking about

the child I had lost.

Zoë Clark-Coates

Day 58

Grief has the power to shatter more than just hearts and, sadly, many marriages break down following the death of a loved one. The primary reason for this is often poor communication, or a lack of empathy for one another.

It is crucial to remember that we are all human, we can all mess up, and we can all disappoint ourselves and those around us with our behaviour. The more tolerant and patient you can be towards one another, the easier the journey to recovery is.

Often men and women can respond very differently to one another in grief. Generally, women are the more emotional party, and men are often more reserved and take on the role of being a protector. However you and your partner respond to loss, communication is the key. Talk about how you are feeling, and talk about the expectations you have of one another, as having to guess what your partner wants you to do or say can quickly become exhausting.

TASK FOR THE DAY:

Make time to talk with your partner about how you are feeling. Tell them the helpful things they have done, which have helped you through this period. Remember, people respond much better to encouragement than they do to criticism.

Hearts break when people
lose someone they love, but
other things can break too:
marriages, friendships, and
so much more.

Zoë Clark-Coates

Day 59

As with any encounters we have in life, there are always certain points that stand out, I guess these are the moments that define our experiences.

I am sure when you think of everything you have been through there are some horrific moments, some tragic moments, but also some beautiful moments. Moments where you were treated with great compassion, or moments where you felt such love and kindness you felt blessed at being cared for by family, friends or medical personnel.

I have had quite a few of these pivotal moments, and just by mentioning them, I can almost feel myself reliving them. One of these moments is definitely being told my baby had no heartbeat. Another is being held by Andy, when I felt myself crumble, when the weight of grief was too much for me to bear.

Talking about these periods in our life helps. Sharing them both helps us, as talking helps heal the memories, and helps others, who may have lived through similar experiences and not felt able to express them.

TASK FOR THE DAY:

Write down what your core/standout memories are—good and bad.

I will forever talk about the babies I have lost because they are part of me and I am part of them. To not talk of them would be as odd as never talking about my living children.

Zoë Clark-Coates

Day 60

I did not know a silent scream existed until I lost my babies, but boy does it exist.

It is a primal scream, a scream that comes from the very core of your being, and I have to say I think it is one of the most painful things to experience, and a highly traumatic thing for family and friends to witness. It can almost be scary to see another person in that much agony, and feel utterly helpless in being able to save them from the pain.

So how can you support someone who is in this much distress?

The most important thing is to let them know you are there and will always be there.

Next, ensure you create a safe place for them to talk and share whenever they feel the need.

Reassure them that whatever they say will be kept private, and ensure you listen, without passing judgement.

Do not worry about saying the wrong things, just be sensitive and consider how things may be taken.

Offer practical support if you can, whether that be cooking meals for their family, cleaning their house, or helping them with other children if they have any.

Let me reassure you that you may feel you are doing very little by just listening, but this can often be a lifeline to those in mourning.

TASK FOR THE DAY:

What are some of the feelings you have experienced in grief that you have never experienced before, and how would you describe them to others?

I didn't know there
was such a thing as a
silent scream until I
lost my baby.

Zoë Clark-Coates

Day 61

So many people wish the world would stop when they are grieving, and I remember feeling this myself. I did not want the sun to set each night, or rise each morning; I wanted time to stop, as that is the only way I thought my pain could go away.

I also wanted to not be acutely aware that the world was carrying on as normal around me. People were going to parties, out for dinner, shopping for the perfect pair of shoes, and I was having to hear about this, when my world was in tatters. I was simply not ready for it.

I think this is what magnifies the feelings of loneliness and isolation in grief. To avoid being told that life is continuing, you have to remove yourself from the world, and climb into a self-protecting bubble. Whilst you are in this bubble you do feel safer, but you can also become quickly cut off from reality, and the thought of re-entering the rat race can be daunting. So if you have retreated to safety, be wise how long you stay there. Regularly try stepping out of the bubble, until one day you feel you will survive outside of the safe cocoon you have built.

TASK FOR THE DAY:

Have you gone into self-protection mode? How are you avoiding pain? Consider how you can start to reintroduce yourself back into daily life.

SOMETIMES IT FEELS LIKE THE
SUN WON'T RISE AGAIN, BUT IT
DOES. MAYBE WE DON'T WANT IT
TO RISE, MAYBE WE PREFER FOR
THE WORLD TO STOP AS OUR
HEART IS BREAKING, BUT IT WILL
RISE AND SET, AND RISE AGAIN.
THAT IS MAYBE THE HARD PART
OF LIFE: IT GOES ON, WHETHER
WE ARE READY OR NOT.

Day 62

If anyone had told me I would be happy again after my losses, I would have never believed it. But I am. In fact, I can honestly say I am much happier today than I was pre-loss.

I used to take life for granted—I do not anymore.

I used to live in the future—I now live in the present.

I used to avoid all situations that could be scary—now I embrace the fear and push boundaries.

I used to be quite inward looking—now I look at the big picture.

Experiencing such raw pain can truly show you a very different side to life, and when you resurface from the dark side of grief, life can be better than before, if you want it to be.

TASK FOR THE DAY:

Consider what you would like to be different about your life, and how loss can help you make those changes.

When you are grieving you are
fully permitted to take time off
from everyday life. You are not
responsible for making everyone
happy. You do not have to try to
fix things. Take time just to be.
Time to sit. Time to feel.
Time to regain your strength.

Zoë Clark-Coates

Day 63

Loss really does make you real. In the darkest days of grief I could not even fake a smile. I was laid bare. I found myself wanting to share my story constantly with anyone who would listen. Thankfully, I knew this was not only normal, it is also the secret to healing, so I never stopped myself.

I did find myself—from time to time—wanting to protect the people I was sharing with. I often saw the look of panic on people's faces when they asked, 'Do you have children?' and I replied with, 'Yes, but sadly they have all died'. In that split second I could see in their faces that they so wished they had never asked, and I was often left comforting them, rather than the other way around. The temptation is to then avoid being truthful and just give non-committal answers to things, but I beg you to be as honest and real as possible. By sharing openly, you are not only healing your heart, you are also helping to break the taboo of talking about loss. You are also showing people that it is okay to talk about baby loss, and you will be amazed at how many people will say to you, 'I have lost too'.

Task for the day:

If you feel ready and able, start a conversation with someone about baby loss. To-gether we can break the taboo.

People ask me if it's hard to constantly be speaking to broken-hearted people. This is my reply: 'It is never hard, it is the opposite of hard—it is easy. The heartbroken don't pretend to be something they are not. They are real. They are truthful. They don't want to impress anyone, they are simply trying to survive.

Zoë Clark-Coates

Day 64

There were times I would sit in my shower, curled into a ball, and sob and sob and sob. As the water flooded over me, my tears would be washed away. In those moments, I struggled to believe I would survive the pain and loss. I felt consumed with raw pain and overwhelmed with grief. I could not even visualise or imagine a time when I would be truly happy, when my soul would feel at peace, and anguish would be gone. What I needed was someone on the other side of the wall, who could speak to me from real experience and say, 'It will be okay, and you will feel happy again'. Today let me be that person for you...

If you want to feel happy again, you will feel happy again.

Focus on today, do not fear tomorrow, just trust that you will not feel like this forever, and believe me when I say the sun will rise for you once more.

TASK FOR THE DAY:

I adore quotes, and it is amazing how hearing these pearls of wisdom can make us feel understood and 'normal'. Find a quote that you love and one that can become your mantra as you heal.

My friend, today may be hard.

Today may feel overwhelming.

Today may feel so hard to face.

You would like to hide under the covers

and will it to go away.

But let me reassure you:

You can survive it. You will survive it.

Take it a minute at a time, and before you

know it, another twenty-four hours will have passed.

Zoë Clark-Coates

Day 65

I often say grief can turn your world to black and white, or it can erase a core colour from your world.

My first three losses erased all colour from my life. It was like that scene in *The Wizard of Oz*, I was sucked into a tornado, landed in a different world, and this world was colourless. It took a while for colours to return, and it did not happen all at once, each colour came back at different times.

With my fourth loss, general colour remained, but some core colours were erased. So it was like green and blue vanished for me. I had to keep life somewhat normal for our little girl, but the world was confused and different, the grass was now red, the sky was now black. Again, it took time for the colours in my world to return to normal.

Grief can be very confusing, and it is different for each person who experiences it, but I think most people will agree that grief is raw, it is surreal and it is utterly consuming. However, grief is a journey and whatever your environment looks like right now, whatever colour is or isn't in your world, it will be a forever changing landscape, so try not to panic if you hate the view, tomorrow it will be different.

TASK FOR THE DAY:

Try to draw a picture of what your grief looks like, or write a story to describe it.

CAN YOU IMAGINE THE WORLD WITHOUT THE COLOUR GREEN? IF OVERNIGHT, THE GRASS TURNED WHITE, FIELDS TURNED BLACK; PEAS TURNED ORANGE? THAT'S A BIT LIKE GRIEF: OVERNIGHT, OUR WORLD LOOKS DIFFERENT. A CORE COLOUR IS WIPED OUT, AND SUDDENLY OUR LANDSCAPE LOOKS SO VERY DIFFERENT.

Zoë Clark-Coates

Day 66

We live in a society where everyone is chasing happiness, and the population seems to constantly state that if you are not happy then something is seriously wrong with you.

Let me reassure you that it is okay to feel sad.

It is normal to have periods of feeling unhappy.

It is part of life to cry, to mourn and to be sad.

In fact, without these things a person will never feel real and true happiness.

Without walking through fear, a person will simply never know what a gift peace is.

How can we know what warmth feels like, if we never experience cold?

So if you feel abnormal, if you feel you are somehow in the wrong for feeling broken and sad, please let me reassure you that you are more than just 'normal', you are experiencing life as it is meant to be felt. Life is amazing and it is awful. It is joy-filled and it is agony. It is good and it is bad, and without experiencing it all, we are living half a life.

TASK FOR THE DAY:

If you feel in the wrong for feeling sad, look at why that is. Has someone said something that made you feel that way? If you can change your thinking, it will make your walk through grief a much smoother journey.

I AM HERE TO SCREAM FROM
THE ROOFTOPS THAT, WHILST THE
WORLD IS TELLING EVERYONE LIFE
IS ABOUT CHASING HAPPINESS,
MILLIONS OF BROKEN-HEARTED
PEOPLE ARE BEING LEFT BEHIND.

Zoë Clark-Coates

Day 67

It amazes me how self-critical we can all be of ourselves. It is much easier to condemn our own behaviour and journey than to applaud ourselves, and give ourselves a much-deserved pat on the back.

I hear hundreds of times a week from the people I support that they wish they could just pull themselves together and get on with it. They berate themselves for struggling not to cry when a person asks them how they are doing. They say that they feel guilty for not looking forward to a special event. What I say to them, and to you, is, 'You are amazing!'

Instead of beating yourself up for not being able to run a marathon at the moment, commend yourself for simply being able to keep moving, even if that is just by crawling on your hands and knees.

You have survived something no parent should need to face.

You are a hero.

Task for the day:

Stop to consider what an achievement it is to survive loss. When you have not even wanted to face one more day, you have done just that. Stop criticising yourself for things you may not be ready to do, and start praising yourself for making it through another twenty-four hours.

FRIENDS, IT'S KIND OF HARD TO BE REAL ABOUT THE PAIN WE FEEL. IT'S MUCH EASIER TO FIX A SMILE ON OUR FACE AND REPRESS THE TEARS IN OUR SOUL. BUT I WANT YOU TO HEAR THIS: YOU ARE TRULY AMAZING. YOU HAVE NEVER GIVEN UP. EVEN WHEN YOU ARE TOO TIRED TO WALK, YOU HAVE REFUSED TO STOP, AND INSTEAD CRAWLED ON YOUR KNEES SO PROGRESS CAN STILL BE MADE. SO TODAY, BEFORE YOU SAY TO YOURSELF YOU SHOULD BE DOING BETTER, THINK INSTEAD, 'I AM A WARRIOR THAT HAS NEVER GIVEN UP'.

Zoë Clark-Coates

Day 68

Society wants us to see the good in everything, and so do many people with a faith. Maybe it is too hard to accept that something could happen and it not have a happy ending. Perhaps we have all watched too many Disney films.

For a long time, I struggled with this whole concept. I wanted something amazing to come from my babies' deaths, but I also worried that this would make their deaths more acceptable and okay … does that make sense?

It will never be okay that my babies died.

It will never be a blessing that they died.

However, their lives have brought me so many gifts, and since their deaths I have been given countless blessings, because they existed.

A person does not need to be born to have lived. The moment they were conceived they existed, the moment they started to grow they had a life.

So perhaps this is how we should look at loss?

We should not look for the silver lining in someone's death, but look for the golden lining of the gifts that have arisen, because they lived.

TASK FOR THE DAY:

How is your life better because of your baby? If you struggle to answer this right now, it may be a question to ask yourself further down the line, but there will be so many gifts that your baby has brought you, or will bring you in the future. These things will help bring back your smile.

Losing my babies will never
be a 'gift'. It will never be a
'blessing in disguise'. What is
a gift and a huge blessing are
the lessons I have learnt since.

Zoë Clark-Coates

Day 69

We all have someone in our lives that makes us feel guilty for being real with our pain.

They are often a person who is significant to us, and because of this, it becomes a challenge, as it is not possible to just walk away from them. In my experience, it is often not about how the grieving party is handling their loss that is the issue; it is actually about the other person's personal views on life and loss. Often it is based in a trauma in their own life; perhaps they lost a baby and never dealt with it? Perhaps their family weren't allowed to show pain, as they were raised to think that tears are a sign of weakness. Whatever the reason they are making you feel guilty, it is okay for you to be real with your pain, and you are within your rights to say so.

How do you tell someone they are making you feel bad for grieving? I would suggest in a gentle way, possibly even in a letter, so you can word it carefully. Focus on how their words or actions have made you feel, rather than challenging the words or actions themselves. People rarely respond well to being criticised, but if you can share how certain things make you feel, it is a lot more likely to be accepted, which could result in behaviour being changed.

TASK FOR THE DAY:

How do you want to be treated and supported? Consider how you can help others to support you in this way.

My favourite kind of people are those that come
into your life and make you see the sun, where
once you only saw clouds. They believe in you
so much, it makes you start to believe in you too.
They love you just because you are you, not
because of what you do or because of what you
own. These friends are the treasures of life.
When you find them, hold on to them.
They are the ones you should do life with.

Zoë Clark-Coates

Day 70

Grief really is like an ultra-marathon. The odd thing is baby loss is also like this. However long it took you to conceive, to go through a pregnancy (of whatever length), and then to lose that baby, it is like running a marathon and then being sent back to the start and told to run it again. Grief can, in some people, increase the desire to have a family, not diminish it, but the thought of having to go back to the start of the race can be truly daunting. I remember sobbing in Andy's arms, saying, 'But we now have to conceive again, then wait for my period to be late, then do the pregnancy test again, then do those first scary weeks of pregnancy again, then go for our first scan again…' The thought of all of this, whilst still grieving, was overwhelming. Sadly, there is no magical way through it. Most people will tell you it is best to just focus on today and not worry about tomorrow, and this is indeed true, but when you want a baby, you want it in your arms now, not in five years' time. Therefore, my advice is to accept it is going to feel truly rubbish for a while, and you will probably feel overwhelmed with a million different emotions and worries. But know that this will stop at some point in the future.

TASK FOR THE DAY:

Take some time to relax, read, listen to music, and allow your mind to be still. Try to stop the endless questions and fears from replaying in your mind, and take fifteen minutes to think of nothing.

GRIEF IS LIKE A MARATHON
IN REVERSE. INSTEAD OF THE
LAST HALF BEING THE HARDEST,
THE FIRST HALF IS WHEN YOU
EXPERIENCE THE MOST AGONY.

Zoë Clark-Coates

Day 71

Often people dread moving into a new calendar year, as the thought of moving into a fresh year, a year where their cherished baby never lived, is just too hard.

Firstly, know that it is okay to feel this way, and it is equally okay to not feel this way, and be thrilled to be moving into a new year. Grief is different for everyone, and what can be a huge issue for one person, is not even a slight problem for another.

What I always say to people who fear time moving on is this: 'Your baby now lives in your heart, you carry them into every day, into every week, into every month, and into each and every year, so you are never leaving your child behind.'

TASK FOR THE DAY:

How would you like to make your baby's legacy live on? Perhaps you can do this by always sharing your story with others. Perhaps you can fundraise in their name. Perhaps you can pledge to never take anything for granted as you move forward in honour of them.

SOME PEOPLE MAY NOT
UNDERSTAND WHY THOSE
GRIEVING ARE RELUCTANT
TO MOVE INTO A NEW YEAR.
THEY SEE A FRESH YEAR,
A NEW SEASON, BUT FOR
THE BEREAVED, IT'S MOVING
INTO A NEW CALENDAR YEAR
WHICH THEIR LOVED ONE
WILL NEVER LIVE IN.

Zoë Clark-Coates

Day 72

Do you hide your pain?

If you do, do you know why?

The most common answer I hear from people is, 'I hide my pain as it is so raw. I am scared to start crying, as I fear if I do let the tears flow, I may never stop'.

Let me reassure you, I have now supported thousands of people and I have never heard of a single one who has not been able to stop crying, in fact the exact opposite is true. Once you release the tears and express the pain, your heart can start to heal. Yes, it is hard to just let yourself go, but I promise you it will help.

Tears are the body's natural release. When we cry we are not only letting out the pain, we are also releasing hormones and chemicals that are created in our body when we are bereaved. So try not to fear, just trust in this natural healing process and let the tears be released.

TASK FOR THE DAY:

Let your mind take you to a painful memory, and give yourself permission to think about it. When the tears surface, do not try to push them down, allow them to flow without reservation.

It is one hundred percent normal to cry for a while, and then to feel empty and almost vacant.

Crying uses all your emotions and can be utterly exhausting. So ensure you give yourself time after you have faced a difficult memory to rest or even sleep.

Some people feel more comfortable doing an exercise like this alone, but others may want someone else there to hold their hand … both are fine.

I grieve for all the
unsaid words that
you will never say.
I grieve that I
will never see you
happily at play.

Zoë Clark-Coates

Day 73

Shock can numb us all for a time, but at some point, the realisation hits that our baby is not coming back. For some that can happen within hours, for others weeks, and for some people it can even be months. When it does hit, it can feel very similar to when you heard the news for the first time that your baby had died, and often people feel they have instantly gone back to square one in the grieving process.

Firstly, let me reassure you, you can never go back to square one in the grieving process. Grief is not like that. Yes, it may feel like you have gone three steps forward and four steps back, but you are always progressing, or remaining still.

When the shock does lift, and you have to accept your baby has gone forever, just allow this next layer of grief to surface, and keep talking about how you feel. Acceptance is a crucial milestone in the grieving process, and once you have passed this point, your brain will be able to process the loss more easily.

TASK FOR THE DAY:

Are you at a place where you can accept your baby has gone? If not, do not try to force it, just be patient and keep talking about how you feel. If you have come to a place of acceptance, try to write a letter or a poem to (or about) your baby, explaining how losing them has changed you.

And one day, not long after, it hit me: my baby wasn't coming back. Every single part of me was consumed with sadness and pain as my heart reluctantly accepted my baby was gone.

Zoë Clark-Coates

Day 74

Feeling alone and wondering if people really do care is sadly a common experience when it comes to child loss. This can happen for two reasons. Firstly, those around you may be struggling to share how they feel, or they may not be supporting you in a way you would like. Secondly, people often shut themselves away after a loss, and this seclusion can promote feelings of isolation and make you feel that other people do not care.

Firstly, please know that people do care. I care, and I know the thousands of people that The Mariposa Trust support also care. So if you do lack caring people around you, please reach out to the charity, so we can support you.

Secondly, I always encourage everyone to consider whether the reason they feel alone is because they have stopped talking about their experience, and because of that, family and friends then feel it is now not a topic they should discuss.

Sadly, people are often afraid to speak about death and loss, and often this means it becomes the responsibility of the bereaved party to lead the way in discussions. Whilst this is extremely unhelpful, and not the way it would ideally be, we have to be aware of it, and at times lead the conversation however much we would prefer a third party to do so.

TASK FOR THE DAY:

Are you still talking about your loss? If not, why not? Are others making you feel you should not? Alternatively, is it because you feel no one wants to listen? Talking is key; it is how we heal. Therefore, I would encourage you to start a conversation today, with a family member, a friend or one of the team at The Mariposa Trust. The key to healing is processing grief, so do not allow anyone to stall this process for you.

AT TIMES, PEOPLE STOP TALKING
ABOUT HOW THEY FEEL BECAUSE
THEY QUESTION WHETHER
PEOPLE TRULY CARE. AS FAMILY
AND FRIENDS, WE HAVE A DUTY
TO SHOW THEM WE DO CARE
AND WE DO WANT TO LISTEN.

Zoë Clark-Coates

Day 75

Many people will not understand your pain, they will not get your grief, and that is okay.

Yes, we all want to be understood, and yes, there is no greater gift than to be heard, and to have our pain and loss recognised, but it doesn't matter if people don't get it.

People not understanding what you have been through, in no way devalues your experience or makes your loss less important. This was such a massive lesson for me to learn.

In the early days following my first few losses, I wanted everyone to understand my pain. It physically hurt my heart if people minimised my loss in any way, but then I realised no one can devalue my experience and my journey unless I hand them the power. It was then I made the decision never to give that power to anyone. I am in control of my story, and because of that, whatever anyone ever says it will not alter or devalue what I have been through or my baby's worth.

TASK FOR THE DAY:

Consider whether you put too much value on what other people think. Are you giving your power away? We can all make a choice on these matters, and when we make a resolution to walk our own path, whatever others may think, it can be truly empowering.

SO MANY PEOPLE WON'T
UNDERSTAND YOUR PAIN AND
THAT'S OKAY. YOU DON'T NEED
THEIR PERMISSION TO GRIEVE.
BE YOU, BE REAL, AND KNOW
YOUR TEARS ARE VALID.

Zoë Clark-Coates

Day 76

The complexity of grief is that we can experience every emotion possible in a ten-minute period. One second we want to be alone, the next we can be craving company. This is when people will often say to me, 'Am I going mad?' Their emotions are so varied, and swing so dramatically they fear they are on course for a nervous breakdown. Let me assure you that this is very normal. Grief is so overwhelming it throws the brain into panic and confusion, making it struggle to know which way is up and which way is down in the weeks following a bereavement.

Because feelings can vary so much in such a short space of time, it can make it incredibly difficult to make any decisions. A simple question like, 'Do you want to go for a walk?', can reduce someone to tears, as it feels overwhelming to decide now, as how will you know how you will feel in ten minutes? And what if you suddenly need to be alone when you are out?

I am afraid there is no secret to helping with this. Just know it is normal, and in time your feelings will level out and this emotional rollercoaster will stop.

If any decision feels too hard to make, say so, and take time to consider your options.

TASK FOR THE DAY:

Take time out of your day to relax. Listen to music, watch a film, but the crucial part of this exercise is, you cannot think at all when doing it. Try to take control of the questions that are flying around your brain, this is your brain's time to rest.

Post loss, it's totally normal to feel
confused and not know what you want.
At times you may long for solitude
but simultaneously crave people to be
around you. In time, your feelings will
become more consistent.

Zoë Clark-Coates

Day 77

The great 'what if' has so much to answer for, and this endless question can make us crave for time to be rewound, so we can do things differently, 'just in case' doing x, y or z changes the outcome.

It is painful to accept time cannot be rewound, and it is hard to accept that in the majority of cases nothing we could have done would have changed our present reality.

If today you are blaming yourself for this loss, can I beg you to stop? Unless you knowingly did something deliberately to cause the death of your baby, you are not responsible, and however much you are blaming yourself *it is not your fault.*

Sometimes it is harder to accept there is nothing we could have done, as that can make us feel even more powerless. It can also make us more fearful, as if we could not have prevented it in the past, how can we prevent it in the future? However, it is important to be real, and it is crucial that you face the truth that you are not to blame, and by accepting this, false guilt can be lifted, and a new layer of healing can be felt.

TASK FOR THE DAY:

Do you blame yourself? How can you get to a place where you do not? A good exercise is try to pretend you have a friend in the same situation as you are now in. If they were expressing their fears and worries and blaming themselves, what would you say to them? Now with that in mind, can you say the same to yourself?

If you can't find the right
words to say to someone
who has lost a baby,
just love them loudly.

Zoë Clark-Coates

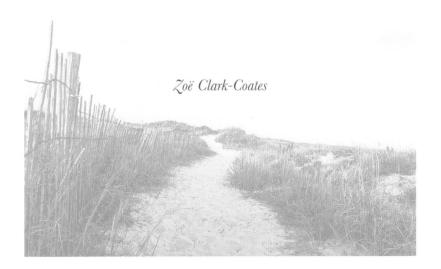

Day 78

It can be hard to accept that there will forever be someone missing from your home.

Whether you go on to have other children or not, one of your children will not grow up in your house. Some people can simply accept this as how life has panned out, whilst for others it is a massive obstacle in moving forward. It can feel unjust, unfair, and some people can even feel a deep anger about this, which refuses to shift.

So how do you accept that your child has gone? For most people talking is the key to being able to accept it, but others need a little more help, and therapy may be a good option.

How do you know if you need more help? Again, this is a hard question, but to answer simply, I would suggest that you need more help if you feel stuck in grief. If you feel unable to accept the loss, and unable to express your pain, which is making the grieving process impossible to move through, a good therapist or counsellor should be able to help. If you're a friend reading this, however, please be aware that you cannot persuade or force someone to get help. It won't be of any value until they feel ready themselves.

TASK FOR THE DAY:

Consider what the hardest thing for you to accept was following loss.

DON'T TELL ME TO JUST BE GRATEFUL FOR THE CHILDREN I ALREADY HAVE. THE MOMENT YOU UTTER THOSE WORDS, YOU ARE TELLING ME I DON'T APPRECIATE MY CHILDREN, WHICH IS THE WORST INSULT OF ALL, AS THEY ARE MY WORLD. SECONDLY, YOU ARE MINIMISING MY LOSS; BEING GRATEFUL WILL NEVER NEGATE THE PAIN AND GRIEF OF LOSING MY BABY.

Zoë Clark-Coates

Day 79

It is okay to think of your baby whenever you want. Society often tells us we need to forget and move on, but this is simply not possible when you lose a child, and the fact is most parents would never want to forget their baby even if it was possible.

When I granted myself permission to think about my baby whenever I wanted to, and the freedom to talk about my baby whenever I felt the need to, it was so incredibly healing. I did not need to do what the world expected or dictated; I could set my own rules. When this reality sunk in, it was exceptionally empowering.

So if you want to talk about your baby, do.

If you do not want to talk about your baby, do not.

You set the rules, remember that!

TASK FOR THE DAY:

Take some time to consider whether you are setting your own rules, or whether you have conformed to the world's expectations.

If you would like to change anything, realise you do have the power to do so.

Don't try to silence your grief. If you do, what started as a purr can quickly become a roar.

Zoë Clark-Coates

Day 80

Panic, and even panic attacks can be common post baby loss. This can happen for so many reasons, but here are a few of them:

1. The trauma of the loss: the brain is struggling to process it.
2. The care or lack of care received during the loss, or post loss.
3. Feeling out of control because of the loss and the feelings that grief naturally brings.

Whatever the reason, panic is a horrid feeling, and this on top of grief can truly push people to the edge.

The most common question I am asked is, 'Will it stay?'

This is impossible for me to answer, but for most people the panic does settle and eventually does pass. For some people, however, it can stay and they may need additional help to break the cycle of panic attacks. If you are worried at all about this, speak to your GP. They will guide you as to what is normal and offer you additional help should they feel it is required.

TASK FOR THE DAY:

Take time to do some deep breathing exercises. Play some soothing music and lay on the floor or on your bed. Next, tense every muscle in your body and hold that for a few seconds, then release and relax.

Be conscious of that feeling you experience when all of your muscles relax. Keep repeating this over the next five minutes, and then stay in that place of being relaxed, whilst deeply breathing for a further five to ten minutes.

You didn't stay long,
but in those precious few
weeks you changed
me forever.

Zoë Clark-Coates

Day 81

A common question I hear is, 'How do you mark significant days, e.g. the days your babies died, or their due dates?' For some people, it feels right to mark these dates on their calendar, and they like to do specific things, like a balloon release. If this feels right for you, I encourage you to do it, as simple ritualistic acts can be helpful. For me, however, I knew I needed to do something different, I knew if I marked these dates on the calendar even once, they would become hallmarks of pain, and I would dread those dates all year. It was with this knowledge I chose to not mark any occasion relating to the babies I have lost in my diary, not the dates I found out I was expecting them, not the dates I lost them, nothing. Instead, I chose to celebrate the fact they lived, every single day of my life. They may have never known life outside of my womb, but their lives changed me, and I want to always remember them with a smile, and never with dread.

I wanted to share this with you, as I know hearing that there are options surrounding commemorating dates can be freeing, as sometimes the world can expect us to mark sad days even if we do not want to. You decide what will work best for you, as only you can determine your walk of survival.

TASK FOR THE DAY:

Think how you may like to celebrate your child. Many people now come to a yearly Saying Goodbye service, which The Mariposa Trust runs around the world. For them, this is a simple and easy way to honour their baby.

I haven't ever commemorated on set days—the date my babies should have been born, or the dates they passed away. I decided from the outset that I would celebrate and remember my children every day of my life. That brought with it such freedom, as I have never dreaded certain points in the year.

Zoë Clark-Coates

Day 82

The added experience of poor care during a loss, or post loss, can add to the trauma of a situation. In fact, it is sadly common for people to say they would have coped way better if the care they had received had been more compassionate and of a higher standard.

This is an area that The Mariposa Trust is committed to improving, and it is working with hospitals, trusts and the Department of Health to better the standard of care offered nationally. Until we get to a place where everyone is treated with compassion and respect, however, we have to acknowledge that how people are supported during the loss itself, and in the weeks that follow, has a dramatic impact on the grieving process and healing time.

If you have not been given the care you would have expected or hoped for, please share that with The Mariposa Trust, it is only when people share their stories that serious issues can be tackled. Also, consider writing to your GP or hospital and explaining where you have been let down. If you received great care, write to them to give them praise.

TASK FOR THE DAY:

What changes would you like to see in the care of parents who lose a baby? Feel free to send any ideas to The Mariposa Trust.

POOR OR NON-EXISTENT CARE
WHEN A PERSON IS GOING
THROUGH BABY LOSS CAN ADD
TO THE TRAUMA. IT IS ESSENTIAL
THAT, AS A NATION, WE COMMIT
TO IMPROVING BEREAVEMENT
CARE IN THE UK AND GLOBALLY.
COMPASSIONATE CARE IS
NOT JUST AN OPTION,
IT IS ESSENTIAL.

Zoë Clark-Coates

Day 83

Guilt for feeling nothing can be common, and if you are one of these people, please let me assure you, you have nothing to feel guilty about. Firstly, no one has to feel specific things; every journey through loss is different. If you feel no deep emotion about your loss that is one hundred percent okay. This book really doesn't focus on this, as my assumption is anyone who has been led to read it, is suffering. It would be lax of me to not include this, however, as I would not want anyone to feel alone if they are experiencing an absence of feelings.

So why would someone feel no great loss? For many reasons, actually.

1. It may be that they see pregnancy in a very scientific way, and do not see a miscarriage as a loss of a life, but more as a natural selection process within the body.
2. Perhaps they see life in black and white terms, and have an ability to accept loss as part of the cycle of life, without it causing upset.
3. Perhaps they have suffered previous trauma, which has left them unable to connect with current trauma.
4. Maybe they are still in a state of shock or denial, so feel nothing now, but will later on.

No one should feel guilty, or be made to feel guilty, for having a lack of emotion, or too much emotion. Each journey through grief is personal.

TASK FOR THE DAY:

Take time to consider whether you judge others on how they grieve or show their emotion. If you do, consider how you can stop doing this, so those around you can be real.

Should I feel guilty for not responding

like other people post loss? Absolutely not.

Everyone's journey through grief is unique,

and no one should be made to feel that there

is a 'right' way to grieve. You set the rules,

no one else—remember that.

Zoë Clark-Coates

Day 84

People are often concerned that if they have another child it will be seen as a replacement child for the baby they have lost. Please do not worry about this, just make people aware this is a sibling for the child you lost. Every baby is unique, and every child is irreplaceable.

Of course, you may experience the odd person who makes a blasé comment like, 'Now you can move on', or, 'At least you now have another baby to focus on'. Any words like this can make you panic, as it can seem like your worst fears are coming to pass. Remember any remarks that others make do not form your reality, they are simply comments from someone being insensitive to the situation. Often the person in question may just be struggling to find the right words.

By having another child, you are purely giving the baby you have lost a sibling.

TASK FOR THE DAY:

Has anyone said anything insensitive to you about your baby, or about your situation? Could you forgive them for saying it? When we forgive those that have hurt us, we allow ourselves to heal, and move on from that pain.

No baby can ever replace another;
every single baby is unique and
precious. Any child that is born
following a baby that has died is not a
replacement, they are just a longed-for
sibling and a gift to their family.

Zoë Clark-Coates

Day 85

Guilt about how you handled certain things can haunt some people.

To be honest, I am quite proud of how I managed to survive my walk through loss, but there are still things I wish I had done differently.

Perhaps it is impossible to come through any traumatic experience and not feel that different choices may have been better. What freed me from the guilt associated with this was the knowledge that I made the best decision I could in that moment, with the emotional reserves I had available to me.

If you can get to a place where you can forgive yourself, or accept that you made the best decisions you could have, given your personal situation or life experience, you will notice a dramatic shift in how you think.

TASK FOR THE DAY:

Consider whether there are things you still beat yourself up about. If there are, forgive yourself and accept that you did the best you could.

SO MANY PEOPLE LIVE WITH
DAILY GUILT OVER DECISIONS
THEY HAVE MADE, AND IT IS
ESSENTIAL THAT THEY GET
TO A PLACE WHERE THEY
CAN FORGIVE THEMSELVES.
HINDSIGHT IS A BEAUTIFUL
THING, BUT WE HAVE TO ALL
TRUST THAT THE BEST DECISIONS
WERE MADE IN THAT MOMENT,
AND ALLOW OURSELVES THE
FREEDOM TO MOVE FORWARD
WITHOUT THE WORDS 'IF ONLY'
HAUNTING US.

Zoë Clark-Coates

Day 86

Fear of trying again. Now this is a topic I could write a whole book on, and perhaps I will, but for now what words of comfort can I offer to you?

The words I know everyone will want to hear are, 'It won't happen again.' Sadly, I cannot tell you this, but I can say, 'I hope it will never happen again.' I can also say, 'Please don't let the fear of it happening again stop you from trying again, if you still have a desire to have a child.' Any life decision based on fear is not good, and it could stop you from getting your heart's desire.

I was terrified of having more children. I did not know if my heart could stand another loss but my desire for a family pushed me forwards and I am so glad it did.

So if you feel ready to consider opening your heart to another baby, my best advice is to look at the many stories of hope, the stories which resulted in a happy ending, and try to believe you too will get to this place. Of course, believing this will not magically make it happen, but I can assure you it will make the journey easier, as a hopeful heart is so much easier to live with than a fearful one.

Task for the day:

How can you make yourself focus more on the positive? Maybe you need to feed your mind with stories of hope and inspirational quotes, or perhaps you need to practise control over negative thought patterns, which send you into a spiral of fear. A great trick is to stop negative thoughts the moment they enter your brain. Try not to engage with them, or even think about them, instantly force yourself to think of something more positive and hopeful. It takes a lot of practise but when you become a master of your thoughts, it truly changes your thought process.

Never let fear make decisions for you. Try to make life choices from a hope-filled perspective, as this will give you the greatest potential of achieving a happy life.

Zoë Clark-Coates

Day 87

Jealousy of others has to be in the top ten of issues people come to me about. They feel guilty for feeling jealous of others who are pregnant, or have babies in their arms. They wish they could just feel happiness for them, but instead they feel resentful that they do not have a baby. So how do you stop feeling this?

For some people it is much harder to get on top of these feelings than for others. For some it is a simple matter of choice. I could not understand why I was left with empty arms, when others had children, but I was acutely aware that I could choose to be happy for them, and could almost force my feelings into alignment. When other feelings surfaced, I simply refused them space in my mind, and chose to be happy for them. In time no other feelings surfaced, I just felt joy for other people.

If you are in the other camp, the struggle can be a lot greater. The thing that will help the most will be time. For some it can take six to twelve months, for others it takes years to get to a place where they can feel happy for other pregnant people. I want to assure you, you are not alone. The feelings you may be encountering are very normal and are sadly just another challenge those who have lost a baby need to face.

TASK FOR THE DAY:

Try to let go of any guilt you feel. You may find it helpful to visualise the guilt as a balloon. Tightly close your hand around its string, and then imagine letting go of the guilt. As you do so, unclench your fingers and imagine the balloon floating away.

Feeling jealous of pregnant women, or families who have a baby to raise, is one hundred percent normal and it definitely does not make you a bad person. You are just grieving the loss of your baby, and feelings of resentment and anger should settle over time.

Zoë Clark-Coates

Day 88

If your partner responds differently to you during or post loss, or they respond in a manner completely different to how you would have wanted, it can be unbelievably hard. Likewise, if your parents or friends respond in a disappointing way it can be very challenging.

The last thing anyone wants when dealing with grief is upset or arguments. On the other hand, it can hugely complicate the grieving process if you are trying to maintain an atmosphere of peace, whilst wanting to be real and honest about the things you are feeling.

My advice here is to pick wisely who you share with. If you have a difficult or unstable relationship with someone, they may not be the best choice of person to open up to daily, as any tension in the relationship may override the help they can offer to you.

Try not to make major life choices when you are in the depths of grief, just focus on surviving the now, and know that there is plenty of time later to make changes if you still feel they need to be made.

TASK FOR THE DAY:

If you could give advice to anyone on how best to support someone who is grieving what would you say? Have you told those around you this? Sometimes it is helpful to friends and family to know how they can support you better, so consider whether this is something appropriate for you to share.

Good support will look different to every person. For one person, excellent support just means having someone available to chat to 24/7, whilst for another, it can be practical support they need. The great thing as family and friends is we don't need to guess, we can simply ask the bereaved person what they need. Remember, every person needs something, and, whatever time you have available, you can be of help.

Zoë Clark-Coates

Day 89

Faith and loss. Whether you have a faith or not, it can be challenging when going through baby loss. Grief is famed for shaking people's belief systems, and everything they thought they knew or stood for can seem shattered or confused. Please know this is very normal, and it is something most people experience.

It would be easy for me to say now is not the time to address the big issues of life, but perhaps there is no better time to consider who we are, and what we believe in. For me loss deepened my faith, it made me more certain than ever that my relationship with God was crucial to my survival. But I know many people who lost their faith when they journeyed through the dark nights of grief.

What I hope you will find is a peace in where you stand as you move forward with life, and that whatever beliefs you have will bring you happiness and the answers you are searching for.

TASK FOR THE DAY:

Do you have a favourite book? If you do dig it out and reread it. Books can be like old friends and can offer a perfect escape from reality, but they can also bring us peace as we hear old familiar words.

WHETHER YOU HAVE A FAITH OR
NOT, LOSING A BABY CAN SHAKE
YOUR WHOLE BELIEF SYSTEM.
PLEASE KNOW THAT THIS IS
OKAY. MAJOR LIFE EVENTS
ALWAYS HAVE THE POTENTIAL
TO DO THIS, AND YOU SHOULD
NEVER FEEL GUILTY FOR TAKING
THE TIME TO ASK BIG LIFE
QUESTIONS WHILST GRIEVING.

Zoë Clark-Coates

Day 90

Guilt for smiling and returning to daily life can be all-consuming. I remember fighting the urge to smile and laugh, as I was scared people would think I did not love my baby anymore. For someone who hasn't encountered loss, that may seem totally weird, but for those of you who have walked this path, I am sure you know that feeling well.

I want to assure you that feeling guilty for smiling is normal, but I also want to tell you, you do not need to feel like this. It is fine for you to smile, to laugh, to enjoy a night out with your friends, to have a wonderful time shopping. None of these things take away from the love you have for your baby, and none of these things mean you are no longer grieving. Our brain loves to take time off from processing grief, and it can be helpful to allow it.

So next time you feel guilty, or next time you tell yourself you shouldn't be smiling, you should be crying … stop. Remember nothing will change the love you have for your child, and by starting to enjoy life again, you are simply taking the gift your baby has given to you, which is a greater appreciation of life.

TASK FOR THE DAY:

If you have been stopping yourself from doing something because you deemed it not appropriate for a grieving person, consider doing it.

Never feel guilty for
smiling post loss. A smile is
not telling your family and
friends you don't love the
baby you have lost.
A smile is telling the world
that your baby has brought
you the greatest of gifts: an
appreciation of life.

Zoë Clark-Coates

So, that's ninety days. Believe me, I wish I could make this 365 days, and maybe next time I will.

Your journey through grief will take a lifetime, but I hope the darkest days of grief are decreasing for you, and if this book has brought you comfort and support, it has fulfilled its purpose.

Remember, your baby will live in your heart for always.

Never forgotten.

Always loved.

Forever cherished.

All my love to you.

Zoë x